HISTORY & FOOD FROM THE BALKANS

Copyright © 2025

All Right Reserved.

Contents

Acknowledgment 1

About the Author 2

Introduction to the Balkans 3

The Prehistory and Classic Period 7

Medieval Period and The Ottoman Empire 15

Formation of The Modern Balkan Countries 24

Complete Bibliography The Balkans From Prehistory to the Modern Era 40

Salads and Sharing's 48

    Shopska Salad 49

    Snowhite, Tzatziki 51

    Russian Salad 53

    Yoghurt with Pepper 54

    Tubule 55

    Romanian Salad 56

    Courgettes with Yoghurt Dip 57

    Fried Aubergine 59

    Pepper and Aubergine Meze 61

Soups And Stews 62

    Chicken Soup 63

    Meatballs soup 65

    Lentil Stew 67

    Cold soup-Tarator 69

    Aubergine Stew 71

    Beans and Sausage Stew 73

    Meatballs Stew 75

    Mackerel With Beans Stew 77

Main Dishes 79

    Chicken Kavarma 80

    Musaka 82

    Yoghurt Eggs 84

    Wine Kebab 86

- Chicken Potatoes 88
- Kapama 90
- Rise with Tomatoes and Kalamata Olives 93
- Serbian Tatar Köfte 95
- Pilav With Chicken 97
- Albanian Lamb Dish 99

Desserts 102

- Croissant Cake 103
- Baklava With Walnuts 106
- Galaktoboureko 109
- Revane, Syrup Cake 111
- Milk Banitsa 113
- Baked Apples 116

Unique Pastries Cooked In The Whole Area 119

- Buhti 119
- Mekitci 122
- Most Famous Banitsa 124

Acknowledgment

This book is lovingly dedicated to my parents, Ivan and Maryia Angelovi, whose steadfast love, guidance, and support have been the foundation of all my endeavours.

To my brother, Georgi, and my sister-in-law, Eva, I extend my heartfelt gratitude for their encouragement and unfailing help along the way.

And to my cherished nephews, Ivan and Marian, whose laughter, warmth, and love remind me always of the truest joys in life, this work is, in no small part, inspired by you.

Huge thank you to the amazing photographer Lucas Georgiev for the cover page. I wouldn't make it without your ideas and to Sasha from Aarhouze photography, for the great food photography.

Without them, these pages would never have found their voice.

About the Author

Delka Georgieva is a Bulgarian-born archaeologist currently based in Britain. Her academic background and professional experience in archaeology are complemented by a longstanding interest in culinary traditions.

In this book, she combines her expertise in the history, customs, and material culture of the Balkans with her passion for cooking, presenting a distinctive perspective on the region's heritage. Through this work, she seeks to make the cultural richness of the Balkans accessible to a wider audience, framed through a Western scholarly lens.

Introduction to the Balkans

The Balkan Peninsula is a region in southeastern Europe known for its complex geography, rich cultural diversity, and turbulent history

Location and Boundaries

- North: Bordered by the Danube, Sava, and Kupa rivers (often considered the northern boundary).
- West: Bordered by the Adriatic Sea.
- South: Bordered by the Mediterranean Sea (Ionian and Aegean Seas).
- East: Bordered by the Black Sea and Sea of Marmara.

Countries in the Balkans (entirely or partially)

Depending on definitions, the following countries are located entirely or partially on the Balkan Peninsula:

Entirely within the Balkans:

- Albania
- Bosnia and Herzegovina
- Bulgaria
- Montenegro
- North Macedonia
- Kosovo

Partially within the Balkans:

- Croatia (southern part)
- Greece (the mainland is part of the Balkans; many islands are not)
- Romania (southern part below the Danube)
- Serbia (southern part)
- Slovenia (small portion in the southwest)
- Turkey (European part, known as East Thrace)

Major Physical Features

- **Mountain Ranges:**
    - Dinaric Alps (western Balkans)
    - Balkan Mountains (central Bulgaria)
    - Rhodope Mountains (southern Bulgaria and northern Greece)
    - Pindus Mountains (central Greece and Albania)

- **Rivers:**
    - Danube River (second-longest in Europe, northern boundary)
    - Sava River
    - Vardar River
    - Morava River

- **Seas and Coasts:**
    - Long coastlines along the Adriatic, Ionian, Aegean, and Black Seas

Climate Zones

- Mediterranean Climate: Along coastal areas (e.g., Dalmatian coast, Greek coast)
- Continental Climate: Inland and northern parts with colder winters
- Mountain Climate: In higher elevations with snow and alpine conditions

The history of the Balkans is complex, dramatic, and pivotal to the broader history of Europe and the Near East. The region has long been a crossroads of civilisations, empires, and religions and has seen frequent conflict as well as cultural blending.

Ancient and Classical Period

- *Prehistory & Early Tribes:* The region was inhabited by Illyrians, Thracians, and Dacians.
- *Greek Colonisation (c. 800–300 BCE):* Coastal areas, especially in modern-day Albania and Bulgaria, were colonised by the Greeks. Classical Greek culture deeply influenced the region.
- *Macedonian Empire:* Philip II and his son Alexander the Great expanded Macedon's power across much of the known world.
- *Roman Rule (2nd century BCE – 5th century CE):* Rome gradually absorbed the entire peninsula. The area was divided into several Roman provinces.

Byzantine and Early Medieval Period (4th–11th centuries)

- After the Roman Empire split in 395 CE, the Balkans became part of the Byzantine Empire.
- Slavic migrations (6th–7th centuries) dramatically changed the region's demographics.
- Rise of the First Bulgarian Empire (681) and later the Serbian Kingdom.
- Christianity spread, dividing into Eastern Orthodox and Roman Catholic influences.

Ottoman Era (14th–19th centuries)

- Starting in the 14th century, the Ottoman Empire gradually conquered much of the Balkans.
    - The battle of Kosovo (1389) was a key moment in Serbian and regional memory.
    - Greece, Bulgaria, Albania, and Bosnia fell to the Ottomans over the next century.
- The Ottomans ruled for 400–500 years, spreading Islam and creating a lasting religious

mix.
- Resistance and uprisings were frequent, especially in the 18th and 19th centuries.

19th Century: Nationalism and Independence Movements

- Inspired **by European nationalism and revolutions:**
    - Serbia gained autonomy in 1815 and independence in 1878.
    - Greece fought a successful war of independence (1821–1830).
    - Bulgaria, Romania, and Montenegro gained independence or autonomy after the Russo- Turkish War (1877–78) and the Congress of Berlin (1878).
- The rise of ethnic nationalism led to tensions between the emerging Balkan states.

Early 20th Century: Wars and Empires Collapsed

- *Balkan Wars (1912–1913):* The Balkan League (Serbia, Greece, Bulgaria, Montenegro) defeated the Ottomans, and then fought each other over the spoils.
- *World War I (1914–1918):* Sparked in Sarajevo by the assassination of Archduke Franz Ferdinand. The Balkans were central to the war's outbreak.

The Austro-Hungarian and Ottoman Empires collapsed, reshaping borders.

Interwar Period and World War II

- Formation of Yugoslavia (Kingdom of Serbs, Croats, and Slovenes).
- Ethnic and political divisions continued.
- During WWII, the Balkans were invaded by Nazi Germany and Italy. Resistance movements, such as Tito's Partisans in Yugoslavia, were significant.
- Widespread atrocities and ethnic violence occurred.

Cold War Era (1945–1991)

- Yugoslavia became a socialist state under Josip Broz Tito, independent of the Soviet Union.
- Other countries like Bulgaria, Romania, and Albania became communist under Soviet influence.
- Greece remained a Western-aligned democracy after a civil war (1946–49).
- Albania turned into a radical Stalinist dictatorship under Enver Hoxha.

Post-Cold War and the Yugoslav Wars (1990s)

- Collapse of communism led to democratic transitions—but also instability.
- **Yugoslavia disintegrated violently:**
    - Slovenia, Croatia, Bosnia and Herzegovina, Macedonia, and later Montenegro and Kosovo gained independence.
    - The Bosnian War (1992–1995) and the Kosovo War (1998–1999) were marked by ethnic cleansing and NATO intervention.

21st Century: European Integration and Challenges

- **Several Balkan countries have joined the EU or NATO:**
    - Croatia, Slovenia, Romania, and Bulgaria are in the EU.
    - Albania, Montenegro, and North Macedonia are NATO members.

Ongoing issues:

- Ethnic tensions (e.g. in Kosovo and Bosnia)
- Economic challenges and political corruption
- EU accession remains a long-term goal for many states

The Prehistory and Classic Period

Introduction

The Balkan Peninsula, nestled between the Aegean, Adriatic, and Black Seas, has long served as a vital geographic bridge between East and West. In prehistoric times, this rugged and fertile landmass was not a marginal zone but a cultural and technological frontier. From the earliest human settlements to the development of metalworking and organised societies, the Balkans played a key role in shaping the trajectory of European prehistory.

This chapter traces the evolution of the Balkans from the arrival of the first humans through to the Medieval Period, exploring how natural geography, cultural contact, and innovation laid the foundations for later civilisations.

Palaeolithic Origins: The First Europeans

The story of the Balkans begins over 100,000 years ago, during the Palaeolithic—or Old Stone Age, when early human species began to populate the region. Archaeological discoveries in caves, such as Vindija and Krapina in modern Croatia, offer some of the earliest evidence of Neanderthal life in Europe. The Krapina site, dating back to approximately 130,000 years ago, is one of the richest Neanderthal fossil sites in the world.

Later, around 45,000 BCE, Homo sapiens began to spread into Europe from the Near East. One of the earliest and most significant findings of anatomically modern humans comes from Bacho Kiro Cave in Bulgaria, where remains have been radiocarbon dated to between 45,000 and 43,000 years ago. These early people used stone tools, hunted large game, and left behind symbolic artefacts, including pierced animal teeth and pendants, perhaps some of Europe's earliest expressions of symbolic thought.

The Palaeolithic Balkans were sparsely populated but served as a crucial migratory corridor, with seasonal movements following rivers such as the Danube. Groups moved through the region, leaving behind flint tools, hearths, and rudimentary art, providing a window into the survival strategies of Ice Age humans.

The Mesolithic Period: Adapting to Change

With the retreat of the glaciers around 10,000 BCE, a period of climate warming ushered in the Mesolithic period, or Middle Stone Age. During this time, the environment of the Balkans changed drastically: dense forests, wetlands, and expanded river systems offered new resources and required new strategies for survival.

Mesolithic peoples in the Balkans developed smaller, more specialised tools—microliths—for hunting small game and fishing. They also began to display more regional diversity, as groups adapted to local conditions. While evidence is less abundant than for later periods, signs of semi-sedentary life appear: shell middens, hearths, and food processing areas suggest longer occupation of specific sites. This period of adaptation laid the groundwork for the next great transformation: the adoption of agriculture.

The Neolithic Revolution: Europe's First Farmers

Around 6,500 BCE, the Neolithic Revolution swept into the Balkans from Anatolia (modern-day Turkey). Farming communities, bringing domesticated plants and animals, began to establish permanent settlements across the region. This marked a fundamental shift in human society: for the first time, people produced their own food, built villages, and developed social structures.

The Starčevo culture, one of the earliest Neolithic cultures in Europe, flourished in parts of modern-day Serbia, Croatia, and Bosnia. Its people lived in rectangular houses, cultivated wheat and barley, and raised sheep, goats, and pigs. Their pottery, often decorated with red and white pigments, signals both aesthetic sensibility and the beginnings of cultural identity.

Building on this foundation, the Vinča culture emerged around 5,700 BCE, centred in present-day Serbia and northern Macedonia. The Vinča people created large settlements (some with over 1,000 inhabitants), crafted elaborate ceramics and figurines, and began working with copper. Most remarkably, they developed a set of symbols—often incised on pottery—that some scholars interpret as proto-writing. These symbols predate the Sumerian script by over a millennium.

The Karanovo culture, based in southern Bulgaria and its related cultures in the eastern Balkans, likewise contributed to the Neolithic tapestry of the region. The archaeological record reveals deep stratification at Karanovo mound sites, offering a continuous sequence of cultural development that is crucial to understanding Southeast European prehistory.

The Chalcolithic Period: Metal, Wealth, and Social Hierarchy

The Chalcolithic or Copper Age (c. 4,500–3,300 BCE) represents the emergence of new technologies and social changes. For the first time, metals were being widely used initially for decorative items, but increasingly for tools and weapons. The Balkans became a centre of early metallurgy, predating similar developments in Central and Western Europe.

This era is best exemplified by the Varna culture, discovered on the western coast of the Black Sea in Bulgaria. The Varna Necropolis, excavated in the 1970s, contains over 300 graves, including one of a man buried with an extraordinary collection of gold jewellery, copper tools, and symbolic sceptres, making it one of the oldest known elite burials in the world (c. 4,500 BCE).

These grave goods reflect a stratified society, with clear indicators of wealth and status. Trade networks extended across the Balkans and into the Aegean and Central Europe, exchanging obsidian, shells, copper, and salt.

The Bronze Age: Networks of Power and Exchange

The Bronze Age (c. 3,300–1,200 BCE) brought new materials, ideas, and levels of complexity to Balkan societies. The alloying of copper with tin produced bronze, which was stronger and more durable than copper alone, fueling the rise of warrior elites and long-distance trade.

The Vučedol culture, centred along the Danube in today's Croatia and Serbia, is among the most prominent Bronze Age societies in the region. Known for its advanced ceramics—including the famous Vučedol Dove (a ritual vessel) and early use of bronze tools and weapons, this culture had connections with both Central Europe and the Aegean world.

Burial mounds, or tumuli, became widespread, often containing rich grave goods and weapons. Settlements were often fortified, indicating a society increasingly concerned with defence and territorial control.

The Balkans at this time were a dynamic contact zone. Mycenaean traders reached northern lands, while northern Indo-European groups moved southward. Cultural exchange, competition, and conflict became defining features of this era.

The Iron Age: Toward Historical Identity

Around 1,200 BCE, the collapse of Bronze Age civilisations across the Eastern Mediterranean ushered in a new era: the Iron Age. Iron tools and weapons, though harder to produce, eventually became more widespread than bronze due to the abundance of iron ore.

In the Balkans, the Iron Age saw the emergence of the Illyrians in the western regions (modern Albania, Montenegro, and Bosnia), the Thracians in the east (Bulgaria and northeastern Greece), and the Dacians in the north (Romania and Moldova). These groups are known primarily through later Greek and Roman accounts, but archaeological evidence supports their cultural and political distinctiveness.

They built fortified hill settlements, engaged in complex rituals, and buried their elites with iron swords, armour, and luxury items. By the end of the Iron Age, the Balkans had moved from tribal confederacies into more structured chiefdoms and proto-states. These people would soon encounter and resist the expanding Greek and Roman.

The prehistoric Balkans were not isolated backwaters but vibrant centres of innovation, exchange, and complexity. From the first farmers to the early metalworkers and warrior societies, the region played a pivotal role in the development of European civilisation.

Too often overlooked in favour of more "classic" civilisations, the Balkans deserve recognition as one of the cradles of European prehistory. Their story is one of continuity and transformation, of movement and settlement, and of a people constantly adapting to a changing world—until the moment when history, as we know it, begins.

Classical Period

During the Classical period, the Balkan Peninsula emerged as a politically and culturally significant region. Situated between Central Europe, the Aegean world, and Asia Minor, the Balkans were home to a wide range of tribal societies and early kingdoms, including the Thracians, Illyrians, Dacians, and Macedonians. This era witnessed increasing contact with the Greek world through colonisation and commerce, intermittent Persian interference, and ultimately the rise of Macedon as a dominant power. The Classical Balkans were a land of both continuity and transformation where indigenous cultures developed alongside new external influences.

People and Cultures of the Classical Balkans

Thracians

The Thracians were among the most numerous and culturally rich peoples in the Classical Balkans. Their territory stretched from the northern Aegean to the Danube and from the Black Sea to the Morava River. Although organised into numerous tribes, the Thracians occasionally coalesced into larger political formations such as the Odrysian Kingdom, established in the 5th century BCE.

Thracian society was hierarchical. Tribal kings and warrior elites controlled wealth and land, while commoners practised subsistence agriculture and animal husbandry. Burial customs included large mound graves containing weapons, jewellery, and imported luxury items, especially from Greece. Thracians had a distinctive religious life, with native deities and cults, as well as clear influences from Greek mythology.

Illyrians

The Illyrians inhabited the western Balkans, from the Adriatic coast into modern-day Bosnia, Montenegro, and northern Albania. Illyrian tribes were known for their martial culture and seafaring skills, particularly their reputation for piracy and raiding during the Classical period.

Social and political organisation remained largely tribal, although the emergence of proto-kingdoms began in some areas. Illyrian warriors used iron weapons and wore distinctive helmets. While they had some contact with Greek colonies, most Illyrians maintained traditional social structures and languages throughout this period.

Dacians

North of the Danube, the Dacians, sometimes referred to by the Greeks as the Getae, were closely related to the Thracians but developed a distinct cultural identity. They lived in fortified hilltop settlements, known as davae, and practised a warrior-based tribal society.

Dacians were noted for their spiritual beliefs centred on a supreme god named Zalmoxis and a belief in the immortality of the soul. Though less politically unified than their southern neighbours, they would later emerge as a powerful adversary of Rome in the first century BCE and CE.

Macedonians

The Macedonians, occupying the northern Greek frontier, were linguistically and culturally Greek, though perceived by southern city-states as semi-barbaric. During the Classical period, they transitioned from a minor kingdom to a dominant power under the leadership of Philip II.

Philip's military reforms, including the creation of a professional phalanx, expanded Macedonian influence into Thrace and Illyria. His diplomatic and military skills enabled him to bring most of the Greek world under Macedonian control. His son, Alexander the Great, would go on to create one of the largest empires in world history, launching his conquests from the Balkans.

Greek Colonisation and Cultural Influence

From the 8th to the 5th centuries BCE, Greek city-states established colonies along the Adriatic, Aegean, and Black Sea coasts of the Balkans. These included Apollonia, Epidamnos, Odessos, Mesembria, and Histria. These colonies served as vital trade hubs, facilitating the exchange of goods and culture between Greek merchants and Balkan tribes.

Greek influence extended inland through trade and diplomacy. Balkan elites acquired Greek goods such as pottery, weapons, and ornaments, while some adopted aspects of the Greek language, religion, and administrative practices. Bilingualism and mixed cultural zones emerged, particularly in regions close to the colonies.

Persian Campaigns in the Balkans

The Balkans played a supporting role in the larger Greco-Persian conflict. In the early 5th century BCE, Darius I and Xerxes I of Persia launched military campaigns into Europe that required them to pass through Thrace and Macedonia. Persian armies subdued various Balkan tribes en route to their main target, mainland Greece.

Though Persian control in the Balkans was short-lived, it introduced new political dynamics. Some Thracian and Paeonian tribes temporarily submitted to Persian rule, while others resisted. These invasions highlighted the strategic significance of the region's geography, especially mountain passes and river crossings.

Economic and Social Development

The Balkans were a resource-rich region. Gold and silver were mined in Thrace and Macedonia, while iron, timber, and livestock were widely available. These goods were traded through networks connecting the Balkans to the Aegean and beyond.

Socially, tribal structures remained dominant, but elite classes grew more powerful and increasingly engaged in international trade and diplomacy. Religious practices blended local cults with Greek influences. Over time, coinage, writing, and other features of Mediterranean civilisation became more widespread.

The Rise of Macedon and the End of the Classical Period

The latter half of the 4th century BCE was dominated by the expansion of Macedon. Under Philip II, the kingdom extended its control over much of the central and eastern Balkans. His victory at the Battle of Chaeronea in 338 BCE effectively ended Greek independence and established Macedonian hegemony.

Alexander the Great, succeeding his father in 336 BCE, used the resources and manpower of the Balkan territories to launch his conquest of the Persian Empire. This marked the end of the Classical period and the beginning of the Hellenistic age. The Balkans, once a collection of tribal societies, were now deeply embedded in an imperial framework that stretched across three continents.

During the Classical period, the Balkans transformed from a marginal zone into a region of major strategic, economic, and cultural importance. While local identities remained strong, the influence of Greek colonisation, Persian military campaigns, and Macedonian imperialism reshaped the political and social landscape. The period laid the groundwork for the Hellenistic integration of the region and its eventual incorporation into the Roman world.

By the mid-2nd century BCE, the Roman Republic had begun its expansion into the Balkans, encountering a complex landscape of tribal kingdoms, Greek colonies, and rising regional powers. Over the next several centuries, the Balkans would be gradually integrated into the Roman world, first through conquest and alliance, and later through colonisation, military organisation, and infrastructure development.

This chapter explores the political, cultural, and economic transformation of the Balkans under Roman rule, from initial contact in the 2nd century BCE through the division of the Empire and the collapse of Roman authority in the West.

The Roman Conquest of the Balkans

The Macedonian Wars

Rome's entry into the Balkans began with the Macedonian Wars (214–148 BCE), fought against the Hellenistic kingdom of Macedon. Key developments included:

- *First Macedonian War (214–205 BCE):* Inconclusive, sparked by Macedon's alliance with Carthage during the Second Punic War.
- *Second Macedonian War (200–197 BCE):* Rome defeated Philip V at the Battle of Cynoscephalae, reducing Macedon's power.
- *Third Macedonian War (171–168 BCE):* The decisive Roman victory over Perseus at Pydna led to Macedon being divided into four client republics.
- *Fourth Macedonian War (150–148 BCE):* Resulted in the full annexation of Macedon as a Roman province.

This marked the beginning of direct Roman control in the southern Balkans.

The Illyrian and Dacian Campaigns

Rome had already engaged with Illyrian pirates and kingdoms earlier in the 3rd century BCE:

First Illyrian War (229–228 BCE) and Second Illyrian War (219 BCE): Suppressed piracy and brought parts of Illyria under Roman influence.

Full annexation came later in stages, culminating in the creation of the province of Illyricum.

In the north and northeast, the Dacians remained independent until the reign of Emperor Trajan, who launched two major campaigns:

First Dacian War (101–102 CE) and Second Dacian War (105–106 CE)

Conquest of King Decebalus and annexation of Dacia (modern-day Romania). Trajan's Column in Rome famously depicts these campaigns in visual detail.

Provincial Organization and Urbanization

Rome gradually incorporated the Balkans into its administrative system, creating provinces such as:

- Macedonia
- Epirus
- Dalmatia
- Pannonia
- Moesia (Superior and Inferior)
- Dacia (after 106 CE)

Later additions included Thracia and Dardania. These provinces were connected by a network of Roman roads, including the Via Egnatia, which linked the Adriatic to Byzantium (later Constantinople). Romanisation progressed unevenly, with some regions adopting the Latin language, law, and customs, while others remained culturally distinct. Major cities included:

- Salona (capital of Dalmatia)
- Sirmium (Pannonia)
- Philippopolis and Serdica (Thrace)
- Naissus (birthplace of Constantine the Great)
- Military Presence and Frontier Defence

The Balkans were of crucial strategic importance to Rome's defence system:

- Major legions were stationed in Moesia, Pannonia, and Dacia to guard the Danube frontier.
- Fortresses and castra (military camps) became centres of urban development.
- Veteran soldiers were often settled in these areas, leading to the growth of Romanised communities.

The region also became a recruiting ground for the Roman army. Balkan-born soldiers, especially from Illyria and Thrace, gained prominence in the imperial ranks.

Cultural and Religious Life

Romanisation brought profound cultural changes:

- The spread of the Latin and Greek languages
- Urban life modelled on Roman cities, with forums, baths, temples, and amphitheatres
- Local elites adopted Roman citizenship, dress, and religion

Religious syncretism flourished. Local deities were merged with Roman gods. Mystery religions like the cult of Mithras and later Christianity gained followers. By the 4th century CE, the Balkans had become a stronghold of Christianity

Several early Christian councils and martyrs are associated with Balkan cities. Notably, Constantine the Great, the first Christian emperor, was born in Naissus (modern Niš, Serbia).

Late Antiquity and the Division of the Empire

In the late 3rd and early 4th centuries, the Balkans played a central role in imperial politics:

- A series of "Illyrian emperors," including Diocletian, Constantine the Great, and others, rose to power from this region.
- Diocletian's Tetrarchy divided the Empire into more manageable regions, with major administrative centres in the Balkans (e.g., Sirmium, Nicomedia).

In 395 CE, the Roman Empire was permanently divided into Western and Eastern halves. The Balkans were absorbed into the Eastern Roman (Byzantine) Empire. However, the region faced increasing pressure from barbarian invasions:

- Goths (in the 3rd and 4th centuries)
- Huns (under Attila, 5th century)
- Avars, Slavs, and others in the 6th century

By the fall of the Western Roman Empire in 476 CE, much of the Balkans was already under the de facto control of non-Roman groups, though Byzantine rule persisted in the south and east.

The Roman period in the Balkans brought dramatic changes in governance, economy, society, and culture. Conquest led to integration, and integration to transformation. While the degree of Romanisation varied, the region was fundamentally reshaped by Roman rule. Its cities, roads, languages, and legal institutions endured for centuries, and its strategic and military importance remained central through the transition to the Byzantine era.

The Balkans, once a frontier of the Republic, became a cradle of emperors and a pillar of imperial power, a legacy that would shape the medieval and modern histories of Southeast Europe.

Medieval Period and The Ottoman Empire

With the permanent division of the Roman Empire in 395 CE, the Balkans became part of the Eastern Roman Empire, later known as the Byzantine Empire. From the new capital of Constantinople (formerly Byzantium), the Byzantines governed this crucial frontier region for centuries. However, unlike in the earlier Roman period, the Balkans during the Byzantine era experienced near-constant military, demographic, and cultural upheaval.

Despite these pressures, the Byzantine Empire maintained significant influence over the region, defending its core cities, spreading Christianity and Greek culture, and eventually reasserting imperial control. This chapter examines the transformation of the Balkans in this turbulent but formative era.

From Roman to Byzantine Rule

The Founding of Constantinople

In 330 CE, Emperor Constantine the Great formally inaugurated Constantinople as the new capital of the Roman Empire. Strategically located on the Bosporus, the city would serve as the political and cultural heart of Byzantium for over a thousand years.

The Balkans, lying directly west and north of the capital, became a buffer zone between Constantinople and threats from Central and Eastern Europe. Key cities such as Thessaloniki, Serdica (Sofia), Naissus (Niš), and Philippopolis (Plovdiv) remained important administrative and religious centres.

Administrative Continuity and Change

Byzantine administration preserved many Roman structures:

Thematic system: In the 7th Century, civil and military authority merged in regional units known as themes, such as the Theme of Thrace or Macedonia.

Local elites and bishops played larger roles in provincial governance.

Latin gradually gave way to Greek as the administrative language.

The Balkans retained some autonomy, especially in remote mountainous regions, but cities and fortresses remained closely linked to the imperial system.

Invasions and Migrations (4th–7th Centuries)

Gothic, Hunnic, and Avar Raids

From the late 4th Century onward, the Balkans were repeatedly invaded:

- Goths (Visigoths and Ostrogoths) plundered cities and defeated Roman forces, most famously at the Battle of Adrianople in 378 CE.
- Huns, under Attila, devastated the region in the 5th Century.
- Avars, a Turkic steppe people, launched destructive raids across the Balkans in the 6th–7th centuries. Despite these threats, major cities often remained fortified and retained some degree of imperial control.

Slavic Migrations and Settlement

The most transformative development came with the Slavic migrations from the 6th Century onward. Slavic tribes moved south across the Danube and settled throughout:

- Thrace
- Macedonia
- Illyricum
- Dacia and Moesia (some abandoned after the Roman withdrawal)

These migrations were not organised invasions, but gradual and often peaceful settlements. Many Slavs eventually assimilated into the Byzantine system, though others formed independent groups and posed challenges to imperial control.

Christianity and Religious Transformation

Christianity spread rapidly through the Balkans during the late Roman and early Byzantine periods. Major developments include:

- The establishment of bishoprics in all major cities (e.g., Thessaloniki, Serdica, Tomis)
- Monasticism, especially in remote areas like Mount Athos
- The conversion of the Slavs (from the 9th Century), often through missionary efforts sponsored by Constantinople

Key figures included Saints Cyril and Methodius, who created the Glagolitic script, later evolving into Cyrillic, helping to spread literacy and Christian texts among the Slavs.

Cultural and Economic Life

Despite instability, Byzantine influence persisted in many areas:

- Fortified towns and hilltop settlements remained active centres of administration.
- Trade networks continued, connecting the Balkans to Constantinople, the Aegean, and the Danube frontier.
- A hybrid Greco-Slavic culture began to emerge, particularly after the 9th Century.

The Balkans became a frontier of cultures, Byzantine, Slavic, Latin, and nomadic—all interacting, often violently but sometimes creatively.

Imperial Recovery and Bulgarian Challenge (8th–11th Centuries)

The First Bulgarian Empire

One of the most formidable rivals to Byzantine authority was the First Bulgarian Empire, founded in 681 CE by Asparukh, a Bulgar leader.

The Bulgars initially settled in the northeastern Balkans and quickly absorbed Slavic populations. Under Krum (r. 803–814) and Simeon the Great (r. 893–927), Bulgaria became a major regional power. Byzantine-Bulgarian conflicts were frequent and sometimes devastating for both sides.

Byzantine Reconquest

Under the Macedonian dynasty (867–1056), the Byzantine Empire regained strength:

- Basil II ("the Bulgar-Slayer") defeated the Bulgarian state at the Battle of Kleidion (1014) and fully annexed Bulgaria by 1018.
- Byzantine administration and Orthodox Christianity were reestablished throughout much of the Balkans.

This reconquest marked the temporary restoration of imperial authority, though new challenges were on the horizon.

The Church and Cultural Legacy

Byzantine religious influence left a lasting imprint:

- The spread of Orthodox Christianity to Serbs, Bulgarians, and Romanians
- The use of Old Church Slavonic in liturgy and administration

Development of monasteries, churches, and religious art across the Balkans

Architecture, mosaic art, and theological traditions were shaped by Byzantine models, creating a shared Orthodox cultural sphere that endured into the medieval and modern eras.

The Byzantine period in the Balkans was marked by both disruption and resilience. While invasions and migrations transformed the ethnic and political landscape, the Byzantine state maintained a lasting imprint through its administration, religion, and cultural influence. Even as imperial control waxed and waned, the Balkans remained an integral part of the Byzantine world, both as a shielded frontier and as a source of new peoples, ideas, and challenges.

The foundations laid during this period would shape the medieval Balkan kingdoms, the Orthodox Christian tradition, and the future political divisions of Southeast Europe.

The medieval period in the Balkans, spanning roughly from the 11th to the 15th Century, was an era of political fragmentation, cultural flourishing, and military contestation. Following the gradual decline of

Byzantine authority in the region, several powerful Slavic and Balkan Christian states emerged, most notably the Second Bulgarian Empire and the Serbian Kingdom (later Empire).

At the same time, new forces were reshaping the regional order. The Catholic West, especially through the Crusades, began to interfere in Balkan affairs. Most significantly, the gradual expansion of the Ottoman Turks from Anatolia into Southeastern Europe by the late 14th Century fundamentally altered the region's trajectory.

This chapter explores the dynamic and often turbulent period between the fall of Byzantine supremacy and the onset of full Ottoman control, highlighting key state formations, cultural achievements, religious conflicts, and shifting power structures.

Decline of Byzantine Control

By the 11th Century, the Byzantine Empire had begun to lose its firm grip on the Balkans due to:

- Internal political strife
- Military defeats in Asia Minor (e.g., Battle of Manzikert, 1071)
- The rise of new local powers in the Balkans and invasions from the north

Despite momentary resurgences under the Komnenian emperors (e.g., Alexios I, Manuel I), the Empire struggled to maintain order in peripheral areas like Serbia, Bulgaria, and Albania.

The Rise of Medieval Balkan States

The Second Bulgarian Empire (1185–1396)

Founded after the Uprising of Asen and Peter (1185), the Second Bulgarian Empire quickly emerged as a regional power.

Its capital at Tarnovo became a cultural and religious centre. Under Tsar Kaloyan and Ivan Asen II, Bulgaria reached the height of its territorial and political influence. The Bulgarian Orthodox Church was reestablished as independent (autocephalous), reinforcing national identity.

After a period of civil war and Mongol raids in the 13th Century, the state weakened and fell to the Ottomans in 1396.

The Medieval Serbian State

The Serbian Kingdom, ruled by the Nemanjić dynasty, rose to prominence from the late 12th Century. Stefan Nemanja (r. 1166–1196) consolidated Serb lands and founded the ruling dynasty. His son, Saint Sava, established the Serbian Orthodox Church in 1219.

Under Stefan Dušan (r. 1331–1355), Serbia became a multiethnic empire, absorbing much of Macedonia, Albania, and northern Greece. Dušan proclaimed himself "Emperor of the Serbs and Greeks" and codified laws in the Dušan's Code (1349), one of the most important legal texts in medieval Southeastern Europe. After his death, however, the Empire fractured, and regional lords (e.g., Prince Lazar) struggled to defend it from Ottoman expansion.

Crusaders, Venetians, and the Catholic West

The Fourth Crusade (1204) shattered Byzantine power and briefly established the Latin Empire in Constantinople. This opened the Balkans to:

- Western feudal lords (e.g., in Latin Greece and Frankish principalities)
- Venetian control over coastal cities and trade ports, especially in Dalmatia, Euboea, and Crete
- Religious friction between Roman Catholic and Orthodox Christians, especially in Bulgaria and Serbia
- Western involvement added further complexity to the already fragmented political landscape.

The Rise of the Ottoman Empire

The Ottomans, originally a Turkish principality in Anatolia, began expanding into Europe in the 14th Century.

Initial Inroads

In 1354, the Ottomans crossed the Dardanelles and seized Gallipoli, gaining their first European foothold. Rapid conquests followed, often exploiting local rivalries among Christian rulers.

The Battle of Kosovo (1389)

The pivotal Battle of Kosovo saw Ottoman Sultan Murad I face a Christian coalition led by Prince Lazar of Serbia. Though tactically inconclusive, the Ottomans gained a strategic advantage. Both leaders died in battle; Prince Lazar became a symbol of Serbian martyrdom in national mythology.

Fall of the Balkan States

Bulgaria fell after the siege of Vidin (1396).

Serbia became an Ottoman vassal after 1389 and was fully absorbed by 1459.

The Byzantine Empire, reduced to Constantinople and its hinterlands, finally fell in 1453.

By the end of the 15th Century, most of the Balkans was under Ottoman control, except for some Venetian coastal holdings and a few mountainous regions.

Cultural and Religious Life

Despite warfare and fragmentation, the medieval Balkans saw significant cultural growth: Tarnovo and Skopje became centres of manuscript production, architecture, and religious art. Monasteries such as Studenica, Mileševa, and Rila flourished.

Both Bulgaria and Serbia developed rich traditions of fresco painting, literature, and ecclesiastical law. The period saw the strengthening of Orthodox Christianity and the development of distinct national churches. Religious divisions between Eastern Orthodoxy, Roman Catholicism, and later Islam began to take clearer regional form during this era.

Legacy of the Medieval Period

By the 15th Century, the Balkans had undergone an enormous transformation:

- Once dominated by Byzantine and Latin Christian powers, the region became part of the Islamic Ottoman world.
- Despite conquest, medieval Balkan identities—Serbian, Bulgarian, Albanian, Vlach, continued to shape future national developments.
- The cultural achievements of this period, especially in law, literature, and church architecture, left a deep imprint on later Orthodox Slavic societies.

The medieval centuries in the Balkans were a time of political volatility and cultural vibrancy. Though threatened and ultimately conquered by the rising Ottoman Empire, Balkan states like Serbia and Bulgaria made significant contributions to European medieval civilisation. This era laid the foundation for both national traditions and enduring regional rivalries, many of which would re-emerge in the centuries of Ottoman rule that followed.

By the late 15th Century, most of the Balkans had fallen under Ottoman Turkish control. The Ottoman Empire, centred in Constantinople (renamed Istanbul), ruled over a vast, multiethnic realm stretching from Hungary to Arabia. In the Balkans, the Ottomans introduced a new imperial system that reshaped society, religion, landholding, and governance for more than four centuries.

Now let's examine the impact of Ottoman rule on the peoples and territories of the Balkans—from administration and daily life to rebellion and reform—and the eventual awakening of national consciousness that would lead to the modern Balkan states.

The Ottoman Conquest and Integration of the Balkans

Completion of Conquest

Following the fall of Constantinople in 1453, the Ottomans completed their conquest of the Balkans:

- Serbia fell definitively in 1459.
- Bosnia was conquered in 1463.
- Herzegovina (1482), Albania (after long resistance by Skanderbeg), and the Peloponnese were gradually subdued.

Wallachia, Moldavia, and Transylvania became vassal or tributary states, maintaining some autonomy. The Ottomans did not destroy local institutions entirely but instead incorporated them into a flexible administrative system.

Administrative Structure

Ottoman governance in the Balkans rested on a combination of:

- Provinces (eyalets) subdivided into sanjaks
- The Timar system, where land revenues were granted to military officers (sipahis) in exchange for service
- Millet system, granting religious communities internal autonomy

This allowed for relative local stability and religious pluralism, though Muslims held the dominant status.

Religious Life and the Millet System

Islamization and Conversion

While the majority of Balkan peoples remained Christian, certain areas saw substantial conversion to Islam:

- Bosnia, Albania, and parts of Kosovo became majority Muslim over time. Conversion was often motivated by social and economic incentives, not force.
- Ottoman tolerance allowed Orthodox Christians, Catholics, and Jews to retain their religious structures within their millets (confessional communities).

The Orthodox Patriarchate

The Orthodox Church was reorganised under the Ecumenical Patriarch of Constantinople, who represented Orthodox Christians to the Ottoman state. This centralised religious authority helped preserve Slavic and Greek Christian identity. The Church played a key role in education, cultural continuity, and ethnic cohesion.

Social and Economic Structures

Land Tenure and Agriculture

The timar system defined rural life:

- Peasants (rayah) worked the land and paid taxes in kind or labour.
- Land remained state property, and private ownership was rare.

As time passed, tax-farming (iltizam) and privatised estates (çiftliks) increased, often leading to peasant displacement and social tensions.

Urban Life and Trade

Ottoman cities like Sarajevo, Skopje, Plovdiv, and Thessaloniki grew into multiethnic centres: Bazaars, mosques, baths, and caravanserais shaped urban landscapes. Balkan cities became nodes in Ottoman and Mediterranean trade networks. Jewish communities, especially Sephardic Jews expelled from Spain (1492), flourished under Ottoman protection.

Resistance and Rebellion

While the Ottomans maintained control through military strength and administrative efficiency, the Balkans were never entirely pacified.

Local Uprisings

Periodic rebellions occurred throughout the early modern period:

Christian brigands and guerrilla fighters known as haiduks operated in rural areas. In Montenegro and mountainous Albania, tribal resistance persisted for centuries.

The Role of Foreign Powers

European states frequently intervened in Balkan affairs:

- Austria and Venice supported uprisings, especially in Serbia, Croatia, and along the Adriatic.
- Russia, positioning itself as the protector of Orthodox Christians, encouraged anti-Ottoman sentiment and rebellion.

Wars between the Habsburgs, Russians, and Ottomans repeatedly devastated the region but also stimulated nationalist aspirations.

Cultural and Religious Identity under Ottoman Rule

Education and Language

Despite limited formal schooling, religious institutions were preserved:

- Liturgical literacy in Greek, Church Slavonic, and Arabic
- Oral traditions, folk songs, and epic poetry, especially in Serbia and Albania

Religious schools (madrasas, monasteries, and church schools) passed down identity and historical memory

The Orthodox Church as Cultural Guardian

The Orthodox Church was central to Balkan identity:

- Saints, martyrs, and feast days preserved collective memory.
- Monasteries like Studenica, Hilandar, and Rila remained active centres of culture and resistance.

The Rise of National Movements

By the late 18th and early 19th centuries, Enlightenment ideas, foreign influence, and growing dissatisfaction with Ottoman rule sparked nationalist awakenings:

- Serbian uprisings (1804 and 1815) led to the creation of an autonomous Principality of Serbia. The Greek War of Independence (1821–1829) resulted in the establishment of modern Greece.
- Bulgarian cultural revival (mid-19th Century) culminated in demands for ecclesiastical independence and national rights.
- Ottoman attempts at reform (Tanzimat, 1839–1876) were too limited to stem the tide of nationalism, setting the stage for the final disintegration of Ottoman authority in the Balkans in the late 19th Century.

Ottoman rule over the Balkans was long-lasting and profoundly transformative. It introduced new administrative systems, religions, and economic structures while allowing a measure of local religious and cultural continuity. However, the gradual erosion of Ottoman power, combined with rising nationalism, foreign intervention, and internal decay, led to a centuries-long process of imperial retreat and the emergence of modern Balkan nation-states.

The legacies of this era—pluralism, memory, religious division, and imperial nostalgia—continue to shape the historical consciousness of the region to this day.

Formation of The Modern Balkan Countries

End of the Ottoman Empire and the formation of the Modern Balkan States

The 19th century was a turning point in Balkan history. After centuries of Ottoman domination, the peoples of the region began to rediscover and reinvent their national identities. Inspired by Enlightenment ideals, foreign revolutions, and local traditions, the national awakening movements gathered momentum, culminating in a series of revolts, wars, and diplomatic struggles for independence.

This chapter explores the ideological foundations of Balkan nationalism, the stages of armed resistance, the role of foreign powers, and the birth of the modern Balkan states: Greece, Serbia, Romania, Bulgaria, and Montenegro.

Roots of National Consciousness

Cultural Revival

In the early 19th century, linguists, historians, and clerics began to articulate the idea of national identity by:

- Collecting and publishing folk songs and epics (e.g., Serbian gusle poetry, Greek klepht ballads)
- Promoting national languages in education, replacing Greek, Ottoman Turkish, or Church Slavonic

- Celebrating medieval heroes like Stefan Dušan, Skanderbeg, and Tsar Ivan Asen II

These efforts fostered a sense of shared history, territory, and destiny.

The Role of the Church and Education

Religious institutions became vehicles of national consciousness:

- The Serbian Orthodox Church preserved language and historical memory
- The Bulgarian Church struggled for independence from the Greek-dominated Ecumenical Patriarchate
- In Greece and Romania, secular schools spread Enlightenment ideas among the urban elite

The Greek War of Independence (1821–1829)

The Greek Revolution was the first successful national uprising against the Ottomans. Led by the Filiki Eteria (Society of Friends), the revolt began in 1821 in the Peloponnese and later spread to Central Greece and the Aegean Islands.

Heroic resistance, massacres, and civil strife marked the struggle, with figures like Theodoros Kolokotronis, Lord Byron, and Laskarina Bouboulina emerging as symbols.

International Intervention

Western sympathy for the Greek cause was strong, particularly in Britain, France, and Russia.

The decisive Battle of Navarino (1827), where European fleets destroyed the Ottoman-Egyptian navy, sealed the empire's defeat.

In 1830, Greece was recognised as an independent kingdom, the first in the post-Ottoman Balkans.

Serbia's Road to Autonomy and Independence

The Serbian Uprisings

- The First Serbian Uprising (1804–1813), led by Karađorđe Petrović, created a temporary autonomous state before Ottoman retaliation.
- The Second Uprising (1815), under Miloš Obrenović, succeeded in gaining de facto autonomy within the empire.

From Principality to Kingdom

The Treaty of Berlin (1878) recognised Serbia as fully independent. In 1882, Serbia declared itself a kingdom, with competing dynasties (Obrenović and Karađorđević) shaping its politics.

Romanian Unification and Independence

Wallachia and Moldavia

These principalities retained local rulers under Ottoman suzerainty but were deeply influenced by Russian and Austrian politics.

- The 1848 revolutions stirred nationalist sentiments but were suppressed.
- In 1859, the two states elected Alexandru Ioan Cuza as joint prince, forming the basis for a unified Romania.

Full Independence

After fighting alongside Russia in the Russo-Turkish War (1877–78), Romania was declared independent by the Treaty of Berlin and became a kingdom in 1881.

The Bulgarian National Revival and Liberation

Cultural and Ecclesiastical Awakening

The Bulgarian National Revival (18th–19th centuries) centred on restoring language, literature, and religious autonomy. In 1870, the Bulgarian Exarchate was established, marking a break with the Greek Patriarchate.

April Uprising and Russo-Turkish War

The failed April Uprising of 1876 provoked brutal Ottoman reprisals, shocking European opinion. Russia declared war, and in 1878, the Treaty of San Stefano proposed a large Bulgarian state.

Treaty of Berlin and the Bulgarian Principality

The Treaty of Berlin (1878) reduced Bulgaria's size and split it into:

- Principality of Bulgaria (autonomous)
- Eastern Rumelia (under Ottoman suzerainty)

In 1885, the two united peacefully, and in 1908, Bulgaria declared full independence.

Montenegro and the Albanian National Awakening

Montenegro

Fiercely independent and mountainous, Montenegro remained de facto independent for centuries. Recognised internationally in 1878, it became a kingdom in 1910 under Nikola I.

Albanian Awakening

Albanian nationalism emerged later, in response to Slavic and Greek claims. The League of Prizren (1878) called for autonomy and territorial unity, but Ottoman and Great Power opposition hindered progress. By the end of the 19th century, Albanian national identity had begun to crystallise, setting the stage for 20th-century independence.

The Role of the Great Powers

Throughout the 19th century, the Great Powers—Russia, Austria-Hungary, Britain, and France intervened diplomatically and militarily in Balkan affairs:

- Russia acted as the protector of Orthodox Christians and Slavic peoples.

- Austria-Hungary feared pan-Slavism and sought influence in Bosnia and Albania.
- Britain and France supported Ottoman territorial integrity to block Russian expansion.

This geopolitical competition often shaped the fate of Balkan uprisings more than local efforts. The 19th century marked the end of Ottoman hegemony and the emergence of independent nation-states in the Balkans. Each people, Greeks, Serbs, Romanians, Bulgarians, Montenegrins, and Albanians, followed a unique path, shaped by their history, religion, geography, and foreign support.

Despite liberation, this era also sowed the seeds of future conflicts: territorial disputes, ethnic rivalries, and divergent national myths. The map of the Balkans was redrawn, but the struggle for unity, borders, and identity would continue into the 20th century and beyond.

At the dawn of the 20th century, the Balkan Peninsula was a powder keg. The waning power of the Ottoman Empire, the ambitions of newly independent Balkan states, and the competing interests of the Great Powers created an environment primed for conflict. The Balkan Wars of 1912–1913, fought over the last remnants of Ottoman territory in Europe, marked a dramatic and violent reshaping of Southeastern Europe. These wars not only redrew borders but also exposed deep ethnic rivalries and paved the way for World War I.

This chapter examines the causes, events, and consequences of the Balkan Wars and analyses their role in setting the stage for the global conflict that followed.

The Balkan States in the Early 20th Century

By 1910, the Balkans consisted of several newly independent or autonomous states:

- Greece, Serbia, Montenegro, and Bulgaria had won or asserted independence from the Ottoman Empire.
- Albania was emerging as a nationalist movement, but had no formal state.
- Bosnia and Herzegovina were annexed by Austria-Hungary in 1908, escalating regional tensions.

These states were driven by territorial ambitions, particularly in Macedonia and Thrace, where ethnic boundaries were complex and contested.

The First Balkan War (1912–1913)

Formation of the Balkan League

Encouraged by Russia and united by anti-Ottoman sentiment, four Balkan states formed the Balkan League:

- Serbia
- Bulgaria
- Greece
- Montenegro

Their goal was to expel the Ottoman Empire from Europe and divide its remaining Balkan territories.

The War Begins

In October 1912, the Balkan League declared war on the Ottoman Empire. Serbia and Montenegro attacked in Kosovo and northern Albania. Greece advanced through southern Macedonia and Epirus, capturing Thessaloniki.

Bulgaria, the largest force, moved into Thrace and fought major battles at Kirk Kilisse and Lüleburgaz, threatening Istanbul.

By early 1913, the Ottoman Empire had lost almost all its European lands except for Eastern Thrace (including Edirne) and Constantinople.

Treaty of London (May 1913)

The Great Powers brokered a ceasefire, resulting in:

- The Ottoman Empire ceded nearly all its European territories west of the Enos–Midia line.
- Albania was declared an independent principality under Great Power supervision.

The division of Macedonia and Thrace left unresolved, especially among Bulgaria, Serbia, and Greece.

The Second Balkan War (June–August 1913)

Bulgaria's Frustration

Bulgaria, having borne the brunt of fighting in Thrace, was dissatisfied with the territorial gains of Serbia and Greece in Macedonia, especially the city of Skopje.

War Among the Victors

In June 1913, Bulgaria launched a surprise attack on Serbia and Greece. This triggered:

- A counterattack by Serbia and Greece
- Romania invaded Bulgaria from the north
- The Ottoman Empire re-entered and retaken Edirne (Adrianople)

Treaty of Bucharest (August 1913)

The Second Balkan War ended with a humiliating Bulgarian defeat:

- Serbia retained most of Vardar Macedonia
- Greece gained southern Macedonia and Epirus
- Romania annexed Southern Dobrudja
- Bulgaria kept only a portion of Pirin Macedonia

Ethnic Conflict and Population Displacement

The Balkan Wars saw the rise of modern ethnic cleansing practices:

- Massacres of civilians, especially Muslims and Albanians, occurred throughout Macedonia and Thrace.

- Refugees, Muslims fleeing Christian states, and Christians escaping Ottoman areas reshaped demographics.
- Nationalism became tied to exclusion and violence, setting a precedent for the 20th century.

Creation of Albania (1912–1913)

Amidst the chaos, Albanian nationalists declared independence in Vlorë on 28 November 1912. The new state was fragile and lacked strong institutions. The Great Powers imposed borders that left many Albanians outside the new country (e.g., in Kosovo and western Macedonia). Prince Wilhelm of Wied, a German noble, was installed as a short-lived ruler in 1914.

International Consequences and the Road to World War I

Austria-Hungary vs. Serbia

Serbia's territorial gains, especially in Macedonia and Albania, alarmed Austria-Hungary, which feared the rise of Pan-Slavism and Russian influence. The 1908 annexation of Bosnia and Herzegovina had already inflamed Serb nationalism. Austria sought to contain Serbia, a policy that hardened into open hostility by 1914.

Tensions Among the Great Powers

The Balkan Wars disrupted the fragile balance of power:

- Russia supported Serbia and Bulgaria, favouring Slavic unity.
- Germany backed Austria-Hungary and cultivated ties with the Ottomans.
- France and Britain tried to maintain peace but were increasingly drawn into alliances.

The assassination of Archduke Franz Ferdinand in Sarajevo in June 1914 by Gavrilo Princip, a Bosnian Serb nationalist, was a direct consequence of this volatile post-war environment. The Balkan Wars radically transformed Southeastern Europe. They ended centuries of Ottoman rule in the region but replaced it with new states whose borders and populations were deeply contested. The violence and nationalism of 1912–1913 foreshadowed the brutality of the 20th century, while the unresolved tensions among Balkan nations and Great Powers directly contributed to the outbreak of World War I. The Balkans had earned its reputation as the "Powder keg of Europe."

World War I shattered empires and redrew the political map of Europe. In the Balkans, where the conflict ignited in 1914, the war brought devastation, shifting alliances, and the ultimate collapse of Austria-Hungary and Ottoman Turkey. In its aftermath, the region witnessed the formation of new states, experiments in democracy, royal dictatorships, and rising nationalism. This chapter explores the role of the Balkan states during the war, the emergence of the Kingdom of Yugoslavia, Greater Romania, and Republican Turkey, and the regional instability that led toward another global conflict.

The Balkans and the Outbreak of World War I

The Assassination at Sarajevo

On June 28, 1914, Archduke Franz Ferdinand, heir to the Austro-Hungarian throne, was assassinated in

Sarajevo by Gavrilo Princip, a Bosnian Serb affiliated with the nationalist group Black Hand.

- Austria-Hungary blamed Serbia and issued an ultimatum.
- Backed by Germany, Austria declared war on Serbia on July 28, 1914.

Russia, France, Britain, and eventually the Ottoman Empire and Italy joined in triggering World War I. The Balkans, already volatile, became one of the bloodiest theatres of the war.

The War in the Balkans (1914–1918)

Serbia and Montenegro

Serbia initially repelled Austro-Hungarian invasions in 1914 but suffered enormous losses. In late 1915, after Bulgaria joined the Central Powers, Serbia was overrun. The Serbian army retreated through Albania in winter 1915–1916, regrouping on the Greek island of Corfu. Montenegro surrendered to Austria-Hungary in early 1916.

Bulgaria's Role

Bulgaria joined the Central Powers in 1915 to regain the Macedonian territories lost in the Second Balkan War. It invaded Serbia and took control of much of Macedonia and eastern Serbia. However, its war effort was costly and unpopular domestically.

Romania's Entry and Defeat

- Romania entered the war on the side of the Allies in 1916, hoping to claim Transylvania from Hungary.
- Despite initial gains, Romania was soon overrun by the Central Powers.

The country signed the Treaty of Bucharest (1918), but rejoined the war just before the armistice.

Greece: National Schism

Greece experienced a deep divide:

- King Constantine I favoured neutrality and Germany.
- Prime Minister Eleftherios Venizelos supported the Allies.

The Allies forced the king's abdication in 1917, and Greece entered the war under Venizelos.

The Collapse of Empires and New Balkan States

End of the Austro-Hungarian and Ottoman Empires

By 1918:

The Austro-Hungarian Empire dissolved, leaving power vacuums in Bosnia, Croatia, and Slovenia. The Ottoman Empire capitulated, its European lands nearly gone except Eastern Thrace.

The Kingdom of Serbs, Croats, and Slovenes (later Yugoslavia)

In December 1918, Serbia united with:

- Montenegro
- Croatia and Slovenia (former Austro-Hungarian territories)
- Bosnia and Herzegovina, and others

This created the Kingdom of Serbs, Croats, and Slovenes, which was renamed Yugoslavia in 1929. Initially seen as a triumph of Slavic unity, it quickly suffered from internal ethnic and political tensions.

Greater Romania

After the war, Romania expanded to include:

- Transylvania
- Bukovina

Bessarabia This created a Greater Romania, home to a large number of minorities (Hungarians, Jews, Ukrainians).

Albania and Bulgaria

Albania emerged from war weak and internally divided; borders remained contested. Bulgaria, defeated and punished by the Treaty of Neuilly (1919), lost territory and faced domestic unrest.

The Interwar Period: Nationalism, Reform, and Crisis

Kingdom of Yugoslavia

Dominated by Serbian elites, Yugoslavia was marked by:

Parliamentary instability

Ethnic dissatisfaction, particularly among Croats

In 1929, King Alexander I established a royal dictatorship and renamed the country Yugoslavia. In 1934, Alexander was assassinated in Marseille by a Croatian nationalist, signalling the deepening crisis.

Romania

Greater Romania tried to integrate its diverse regions but faced ethnic discontent and rising fascism, notably the Iron Guard. King Carol II dissolved parliament in 1938 and imposed authoritarian rule.

Bulgaria

Lost its territorial ambitions but remained revanchist. Experienced coups, social unrest, and eventually a monarchist-fascist government under Tsar Boris III.

Greece

Greece expanded in the Greco-Turkish War (1919–1922), but suffered a catastrophic defeat at Smyrna, resulting in a massive population exchange with Turkey. In the 1930s, General Ioannis Metaxas established a royalist authoritarian regime (1936).

Albania

Weak institutions led to Ahmet Zogu declaring himself King Zog I in 1928. Albania relied increasingly on Italian support, compromising its independence.

Ethnic Minorities and Rising Tensions

The interwar period saw:

- Forced population movements (notably the 1923 Greek-Turkish exchange)
- Repression of minorities, including Turks, Jews, and Slavs.
- Increasing antisemitism, especially in Romania and Bulgaria
- Ethnic tensions were exacerbated by economic hardship and authoritarian nationalism.

Toward War Again: The Balkans in the Late 1930s

By the late 1930s:

The Balkans were politically fragile and increasingly influenced by Germany and Italy. Axis-aligned regimes emerged in Romania, Bulgaria, and Albania. Yugoslavia and Greece tried to remain neutral but were surrounded by enemies and internal instability. The outbreak of World War II in 1939 would again engulf the region in violence, occupation, and revolution.

The First World War and its aftermath transformed the Balkans beyond recognition. Empires collapsed, new nations emerged, and the hope of unity was often drowned by ethnic division, political extremism, and foreign manipulation. The interwar period offered glimpses of democracy but was ultimately defined by crises of identity and legitimacy, paving the way for totalitarianism, war, and genocide in the next decade.

The Balkans once again became a central stage for geopolitical conflict during World War II. From 1941 to 1945, the region was invaded, occupied, and carved up by the Axis powers. Puppet regimes were established, ethnic violence exploded, and resistance movements emerged with revolutionary consequences.

Unlike much of Europe, the Balkans were engulfed not only in foreign occupation but also in civil wars, genocide, and ideological struggle. The war fundamentally reshaped the region's political future, laying the groundwork for Communist rule, Cold War divisions, and long-standing ethnic grievances.

The Axis Invasion and Partition of the Balkans

Italy Invades Greece (1940)

In October 1940, Fascist Italy invaded Greece from occupied Albania. The Greek army repelled the attack and counter-invaded Albania. This Italian failure prompted Germany to intervene in the Balkans.

Yugoslavia Overthrown (March–April 1941)

In March 1941, the Yugoslav government joined the Axis under pressure. Days later, a British-supported coup overthrew the government. In retaliation, Germany invaded Yugoslavia on 6 April 1941, alongside

Italy, Hungary, and Bulgaria.

The German Blitzkrieg

Yugoslavia surrendered in 11 days. Greece also fell after a rapid German offensive through Macedonia. British and Commonwealth forces were evacuated to Crete, which soon fell to German paratroopers. Occupation and Partition of the Balkans

The Balkans were carved into various Axis zones of occupation: Yugoslavia, Germany, Italy, Hungary, and Bulgaria occupied different regions. The Independent State of Croatia (NDH) was created as a fascist puppet regime, led by the Ustaše, a violent ultranationalist movement. Serbia was ruled by a German-controlled puppet government under Milan Nedić. Montenegro became an Italian protectorate.

Greece

Divided into German, Italian, and Bulgarian occupation zones. Harsh conditions and famine plagued Greek cities, especially Athens.

Albania and Bulgaria

- Albania, enlarged with Kosovo and parts of Macedonia, was an Italian client state.
- Bulgaria, an Axis ally, annexed parts of Macedonia, Thrace, and Serbia.

Genocide and Ethnic Violence

The Holocaust in the Balkans

Jewish communities in Greece, Yugoslavia, and Bulgaria were targeted. In Greece, especially Thessaloniki, the majority of Sephardic Jews were deported to Auschwitz. In Croatia, the Ustaše regime established Jasenovac, a concentration camp where tens of thousands of Serbs, Jews, and Roma were murdered.

Bulgaria deported Jews from occupied territories (e.g. Thrace and Macedonia), though Jews within Bulgaria proper were spared due to the incredible protective role of Tsar Boris III

Interethnic Violence and Civil Conflict

Ustaše massacred Serbs, Jews, and Roma in Croatia and Bosnia.

In turn, Chetnik forces (Serbian royalist guerrillas) committed reprisals against Muslims and Croats. In Bosnia, Muslim militias and German-backed SS units were involved in atrocities. The lines between occupation, civil war, and ethnic cleansing were often blurred.

Resistance Movements

Yugoslavia: Chetniks and Partisans

The Chetniks, royalist Serb forces under Draža Mihailović, initially resisted but increasingly collaborated with Axis forces to fight communists.

The Partisans, led by Josip Broz Tito, launched a multi-ethnic, communist resistance. Gained support due to effective guerrilla warfare and inclusive ideology. Received British and Soviet support after 1943. By 1945, the Partisans controlled most of Yugoslavia and had emerged as its new ruling force.

Greece: EAM-ELAS and EDES

EAM-ELAS, the communist-led resistance, became the largest anti-Axis force in Greece. EDES, a republican group, also resisted but eventually clashed with EAM. After liberation, civil conflict between these factions foreshadowed the Greek Civil War (1946–1949).

Albania: Communist Victory

Albanian partisans, led by Enver Hoxha, defeated Italian and German occupiers. With minimal foreign support, Hoxha's forces took control and established a communist dictatorship.

Allied Strategy and Liberation Shifting Support

Initially, the Allies supported royalist resistance movements. By 1943–44, Churchill and Stalin agreed to back Tito and Hoxha due to their effectiveness. Greece was placed under British influence, Yugoslavia and Albania under Soviet spheres.

Liberation and Retreat of Axis Powers

As Germany weakened, local partisan forces, with Red Army assistance, liberated: Yugoslavia (late 1944) Bulgaria (which switched sides in 1944) Albania, Northern Greece, where the British returned to enforce order. The Axis retreat was accompanied by massacres, political executions, and the beginning of postwar purges.

The End of the War and the New Balkan Order Rise of Communist States

By 1945, Communist regimes had taken power in: Yugoslavia (Tito)

Albania (Hoxha)

Bulgaria, under Soviet guidance Greece: Into Civil War

The British-backed monarchy clashed with the leftist EAM-ELAS. A civil war erupted in 1946, dragging Greece into the early Cold War.

Demographic Shifts and Expulsions

Millions were displaced:

Jews, Serbs, Greeks, Turks, and ethnic Germans were expelled or fled. The region's ethnic landscape was radically altered. World War II in the Balkans was more than a confrontation between Axis and Allies—it was a multifaceted catastrophe involving occupation, genocide, ideological warfare, and national revolution. The region suffered immensely, but out of the rubble rose a new political order dominated by Communism in the north and a fragile monarchy in the south.

The legacies of wartime collaboration, resistance, and civil conflict would deeply influence the Cold

War era, the shape of Balkan societies, and the enduring memory of violence well into the 21st century.

In the aftermath of World War II, the Balkans became sharply divided between Communist regimes aligned with the Soviet Union and Western-aligned states. This division laid the foundation for the region's transformation throughout the Cold War era. Nationalisation, repression, ideological reform, and foreign alignment defined the politics of the time.

While the countries of the region shared certain commonalities under Communism, their experiences were far from uniform. From Tito's independent socialism in Yugoslavia to Hoxha's paranoid autocracy in Albania, the Cold War era was one of stark contrasts, periodic upheavals, and deep social transformation.

The Postwar Settlement and Communist Takeover

Soviet Influence and the Iron Curtain

In the wake of World War II, the Soviet Union exerted strong influence over Eastern Europe, including Bulgaria, Romania, and parts of Yugoslavia. Albania, while not directly occupied, fell under Communist control with Enver Hoxha's partisans. Greece, however, was spared from Communist rule after a British-backed intervention and a brutal civil war.

Communist Takeovers

Bulgaria, Romania, and Albania saw monarchies abolished and People's Republics declared between 1946 and 1947.

Deviation from Moscow

Initially a Stalinist state, Romania under Gheorghe Gheorghiu-Dej began distancing itself from the USSR in the 1960s. Nicolae Ceaușescu, who came to power in 1965, pursued a policy of national communism and independence from Soviet control. The Ceaușescu Regime Ceaușescu promoted a cult of personality Massive industrialisation

Surveillance by the Securitate

His 1980s austerity program, designed to repay foreign debt, devastated living standards. Albania: Isolation and Totalitarianism

Hoxha's Stalinism

Enver Hoxha ruled from 1944 to 1985 with brutal repression and total ideological control. He severed ties with:

- Yugoslavia (1948)
- Soviet Union (1961)
- China (1978)

Albania became Europe's most isolated country, resembling North Korea in many respects.

Total Control

Religion was banned (Albania declared the first atheist state in 1967). Citizens lived under constant surveillance and isolation. The country was filled with concrete bunkers, symbolising its paranoia. Greece: From Civil War to NATO Ally

Greek Civil War (1946–1949)

The civil war between royalist and communist forces resulted in victory for the monarchist government, supported by Britain and the U.S. Greece joined NATO in 1952, firmly aligning with the West.

Military Junta (1967–1974)

In 1967, a right-wing military coup established a dictatorship, known as the Regime of the Colonels. The regime collapsed in 1974 after the Turkish invasion of Cyprus. Greece restored democracy and abolished the monarchy in 1975.

Social and Economic Transformations

Industrialisation and Urbanisation

Communist states invested heavily in heavy industry, often ignoring consumer goods. Massive urban migration transformed social life but strained infrastructure.

Education and Women's Rights

Literacy campaigns and universal education improved human development. Women were integrated into the workforce, though genuine equality varied. Surveillance and Dissent Secret police and party informants monitored citizens. Dissidents faced imprisonment, exile, or execution. Intellectuals, artists, and clergy often navigated a fine line between cooperation and resistance.

Cracks in the System (1980s)

Economic Decline

By the 1980s, most Balkan communist states faced:

- Debt crises Shortages
- Public discontent
- Tito's death in 1980 weakened Yugoslavia's cohesion.

Cultural Revival and Nationalism

Relaxation of control allowed suppressed ethnic identities and religious expression to reemerge. In Yugoslavia, this would soon fuel ethnic separatism.

The Cold War shaped the Balkans into a zone of ideological contrast, repression, and transformation. Communist regimes brought literacy, industrialisation, and some stability—but at a high cost in terms of freedom, pluralism, and national autonomy.

By the late 1980s, the model of governance across the Balkans was in crisis. The stage was set for the dramatic collapses of 1989–1991, which would dissolve not only regimes but entire states, and launch the region into yet another period of profound upheaval.

The final decade of the 20th century was one of seismic political, social, and humanitarian upheaval in the Balkans. As Communist regimes collapsed across Eastern Europe in 1989–1991, the Balkans faced not only a transformation of governance but also the violent unravelling of Yugoslavia, the rise of new nation-states, and some of the worst atrocities in Europe since World War II. This chapter examines the fall of Communism in the Balkans, the complex and violent disintegration of Yugoslavia, and the international community's response to the wars in Croatia, Bosnia, and Kosovo.

The Fall of Communism in the Balkans

Peaceful Transitions

Bulgaria:

Communist leader Todor Zhivkov was ousted in 1989. A multi-party system emerged, and democratic reforms were enacted.

Romania:

The most violent transition. In December 1989, Nicolae Ceaușescu and his wife were tried and executed after a popular uprising.

Albania:

Following student protests and mounting unrest, the regime of Ramiz Alia (Hoxha's successor) collapsed by 1991.

Yugoslavia's Fragile Unity

After Tito's death (1980), economic decline, rising nationalism, and a weak federal system led to instability. By 1989, Slobodan Milošević emerged as a powerful nationalist figure in Serbia, undermining federal cohesion.

The Breakup of Yugoslavia

Rise of Nationalism

Republican leaders in Croatia, Slovenia, Bosnia, and Macedonia sought greater autonomy or independence. Serbia, under Milošević, aimed to centralise power and preserve Yugoslavia under Serbian dominance.

Declarations of Independence

Slovenia and Croatia declared independence in June 1991. Bosnia and Herzegovina followed in March 1992. Macedonia declared independence peacefully in 1991, though Greece objected to its name.

Wars of Yugoslav Succession

The Ten-Day War in Slovenia (1991)

A brief conflict between Slovenian forces and the Yugoslav People's Army (JNA). Ended quickly with Slovenia's effective secession.

The Croatian War of Independence (1991–1995)

Ethnic Serbs in Croatia, backed by Belgrade, rebelled against Croatian independence. The war saw:

Siege of Vukovar

Ethnic cleansing of Croats from Serb-held areas Expulsions of Serbs during Operation Storm in 1995

The Bosnian War (1992–1995)

One of the most devastating conflicts of the post-WWII era:

Bosnia was a multiethnic republic of Bosniaks (Muslims), Croats, and Serbs. After independence, Bosnian Serbs, backed by Serbia, launched a war to create a "Greater Serbia." Key atrocities included:

Siege of Sarajevo (1992–1996)

Srebrenica massacre (1995), where over 8,000 Bosniak men and boys were murdered Massive displacement and ethnic cleansing. The international community, after prolonged inaction, intervened with NATO air strikes in 1995, leading to the Dayton Accords.

The Kosovo Conflict (1998–1999) Background

- Kosovo, a majority-Albanian province of Serbia, sought autonomy or independence.
- Serbian repression intensified in the 1990s, leading to the rise of the Kosovo Liberation Army (KLA).

Humanitarian Crisis and NATO Intervention

- In 1998–1999, Serbian forces launched a brutal campaign of massacres and deportations. Over 800,000 Kosovars were displaced.
- NATO intervened without UN authorisation, launching air strikes against Serbia in March 1999.
- Slobodan Milošević capitulated in June 1999, and Kosovo was placed under UN administration.

International Responses and War Crimes

The International Criminal Tribunal for the former Yugoslavia (ICTY) Established in 1993 at The Hague. Indicted key figures including:

- Slobodan Milošević Radovan Karadžić Ratko Mladić
- Delivered landmark rulings on genocide, ethnic cleansing, and sexual violence as tools of war.

Peace Agreements

- Dayton Accords (1995) ended the Bosnian War, creating a complex power-sharing system.
- Kumanovo Agreement (1999) ended the Kosovo conflict, with NATO presence maintained in the region.

The Human Cost and Legacy

An estimated 140,000+ deaths from the Yugoslav wars. Millions were displaced as refugees or internally displaced persons (IDPs). Deep trauma, destroyed infrastructure, and polarised communities left a lasting legacy. Greece and Bulgaria in the 1990s

Greece

Stable democracy, but embroiled in diplomatic tensions with Macedonia over the latter's name. Supported international efforts in Bosnia and Kosovo with reservations.

Bulgaria

Transitioned peacefully to democracy and a market economy. Hosted refugees from neighbouring Yugoslavia. Sought Euro-Atlantic integration, joining NATO in 2004.

The 1990s were a decade of profound fracture and violence in the Balkans. The dissolution of Yugoslavia released suppressed national tensions with devastating consequences. While other Balkan nations transitioned relatively peacefully, the wars in Croatia, Bosnia, and Kosovo became synonymous with modern ethnic conflict and humanitarian tragedy.

The international community's slow and inconsistent response left scars on regional memory. By the decade's end, a fragile peace had returned—but the political, social, and emotional divisions created during this time would shape the 21st-century Balkans.

Complete Bibliography
The Balkans From Prehistory to the Modern Era

Prehistoric and Early Farming Communities

Chapman, John. "Social Power in the Early Farming Communities of Eastern and Central Europe: The Evidence of Longhouses." *Archaeological Review from Cambridge* 9, no. 1 (1990): 35–47.

Lichardus, Jan, and Magdalena Lichardus-Itten. "The Balkans in the 6th and 5th Millennia B.C.: The Vinča Culture and Its Neighbours." *Documenta Praehistorica* 23 (1996): 141–156.

Manolakakis, Loukas. "Social Complexity and Inequality in the Neolithic Balkans: A View from the Southern Balkans." *Documenta Praehistorica* 38 (2011): 219–232.

Higham, Tom et al. "Radiocarbon Dating of Neolithic Settlements in Southeast Europe: New Dates for the Vinča Culture." *Antiquity* 88, no. 341 (2014): 1–15.

Copper Age and Early Metallurgy

Renfrew, Colin, and Marija Gimbutas. "Varna and the Emergence of Wealth in Prehistoric Europe." *Scientific American* 266, no. 4 (1992): 100–107.

Radivojević, Miljana, and Thilo Rehren. "Origins of Metallurgy in the Balkans: A Review of Evidence from the 5th and 6th Millennia BC." *Journal of Archaeological Science* 36, no. 5 (2009): 903–913.

Radivojević, Miljana et al. "On the Origins of Extractive Metallurgy: New Evidence from Europe." *Journal of Archaeological Science* 37, no. 11 (2010): 2775–2787.

Bronze and Iron Ages

Gavranović, M. et al. "Bronze Age Metallurgy in the Central Balkans: The Role of the Vatin Culture in Regional Exchange Networks." *Journal of Archaeological Science: Reports* 31 (2020): 102356.

Harding, Anthony. "Trade and Exchange in Bronze Age Europe: The Case of the Balkans." *European Journal of Archaeology* 6, no. 2 (2003): 119–134.

Stojić, Milorad. "Social Structure and Warfare in the Iron Age Western Balkans: A Case Study from the Glasinac Culture." *Balcanica* 43 (2012): 21–43.

General and Comparative Studies (Prehistory)

Tringham, Ruth, and Mirjana Stevanović. "Engendered Places in Prehistory." In *Gender and Material Culture in Archaeological Perspective*, edited by Moira Donald and Linda Hurcombe, Macmillan, 2000, pp. 170–203.

Whittle, Alasdair. "Time, Tradition and Society in South-East European Neolithic." *Antiquity* 73, no. 281 (1999): 849–864.

Classical Period

Andraste, Marcus. *The Thracians: History and Culture of a Tribal Empire*. London: Thames & Hudson, 2011.

Boardman, John. *The Greeks Overseas: Their Early Colonies and Trade*. 4th ed. London: Thames & Hudson, 1999.

Borza, Eugene N. *In the Shadow of Olympus: The Emergence of Macedon*. Princeton: Princeton University Press, 1990.

Fol, Alexander. *Thracian Culture and the Thracians*. London: Zed Books, 1986.

Freeman, Philip. *The Philosopher and the Druids: A Journey Among the Ancient Celts*. New York: Simon & Schuster, 2006.

Hammond, N. G. L. *A History of Macedonia. Volume II: 550–336 B.C.* Oxford: Clarendon Press, 1979.

Harding, Anthony. *The Archaeology of Celtic Art*. London: Routledge, 2007.

Katičić, Radoslav. *Ancient Languages of the Balkans*. The Hague: Mouton, 1976.

Papazoglu, Fanula. *The Central Balkan Tribes in Pre-Roman Times*. Amsterdam: Hakkert, 1978.

Petković, Slobodan. *The Illyrians and Their Neighbours: Cultural Interactions in the Western Balkans*. Belgrade: Institute of Balkan Studies, 2004.

Roisman, Joseph, and Ian Worthington, eds. *A Companion to Ancient Macedonia*. Malden, MA: Wiley-Blackwell, 2010.

Srejović, Dragoslav. *The Illyrians and the Thracians*. Belgrade: Jugoslavija Publishing, 1982.

Tsetskhladze, Gocha R. *Greek Colonisation: An Account of Greek Colonies and Other Settlements Overseas. Volume I*. Leiden: Brill, 2006.

Zirra, Vasile. "The Dacians and Their Fortified Settlements." In *The Cambridge Ancient History*, Vol. 10. Cambridge: Cambridge University Press, 1996.

Roman Period

Alföldy, Géza. *The Social History of Rome*. London: Croom Helm, 1985.

Batlorić, Marija. *Roman Dacia: Conquest and Provincial Organisation*. Bucharest: Romanian Academy Press, 2004.

Bowman, Alan K., Edward Champlin, and Andrew Lintott, eds. *The Cambridge Ancient History: Volume 10, The Augustan Empire, 43 B.C.–A.D. 69*. Cambridge: Cambridge University Press, 1996.

Davies, John. *The Roman Empire: A Very Short Introduction*. Oxford: Oxford University Press, 2000.
Diaconescu, Alexandru. *Dacia Felix: Romanisation and Urban Life in Roman Dacia*. Cluj-Napoca: Cluj University Press, 2012.

Grant, Michael. *The History of Rome*. London: Faber & Faber, 1993.

Greenhalgh, Peter. *Pompey's Balkan Campaigns*. Ithaca: Cornell University Press, 1997.

Hammond, N. G. L. *Epirus: The Geography, the Ancient Remains, the History and Topography of Epirus and Adjacent Areas*. Oxford: Clarendon Press, 1967.

Heather, Peter. *The Fall of the Roman Empire: A New History*. London: Macmillan, 2005.

Jones, A. H. M. *The Later Roman Empire, 284–602: A Social, Economic and Administrative Survey*. 2 vols. Oxford: Blackwell, 1964.

Mattingly, David. *Imperialism, Power, and Identity: Experiencing the Roman Empire*. Princeton: Princeton University Press, 2010.

Mócsy, András. *Pannonia and Upper Moesia: A History of the Middle Danube Provinces of the Roman Empire*. Translated by S. Frere. London: Routledge, 1974.

Papazoglou, Fanoula. *The Central Balkan Tribes in Pre-Roman Times*. Amsterdam: Hakkert, 1978.

Petković, Slobodan. *The Roman Balkans: From Conquest to Collapse*. Belgrade: Institute for Balkan Studies, 2011.

Srejović, Dragoslav. *The Roman Empire and the Balkans: Cultural and Military Contacts*. Belgrade: Serbian Academy of Sciences, 1982.

Todorova, Henrieta. *Roman Provinces in the Balkans: Culture, Economy, and Administration*. Sofia: Bulgarian Academy of Sciences, 1999.

Wilkes, J. J. *The Illyrians*. Oxford: Blackwell, 1992.

Zanker, Paul. *The Power of Images in the Age of Augustus*. Ann Arbor: University of Michigan Press, 1988.

Byzantine and Medieval Balkans

Avramea, Anastasia. "Land and Sea Communications, Fourth–Fifteenth Centuries." In *The Economic History of Byzantium*, edited by Angeliki E. Laiou, 57–90. Washington, DC: Dumbarton Oaks, 2002.

Curta, Florin. *Southeastern Europe in the Middle Ages, 500–1250*. Cambridge: Cambridge University Press, 2006.

Dvornik, Francis. *The Slavs in European History and Civilisation*. New Brunswick, NJ: Rutgers University Press, 1962.

Fine, John V. A. *The Early Medieval Balkans: A Critical Survey from the Sixth to the Late Twelfth Century*. Ann Arbor: University of Michigan Press, 1983.

Fine, John V. A. *The Late Medieval Balkans: A Critical Survey from the Late Twelfth Century to the Ottoman Conquest*. Ann Arbor: University of Michigan Press, 1987.

Golden, Peter B. *An Introduction to the History of the Turkic Peoples: Ethnogenesis and State Formation in Medieval and Early Modern Eurasia and the Middle East.* Wiesbaden: Otto Harrassowitz, 1992.

Haldon, John. *The Byzantine Wars: Battles and Campaigns of the Byzantine Era.* Stroud: Tempus, 2001.

Herrin, Judith. *Byzantium: The Surprising Life of a Medieval Empire.* London: Penguin Books, 2007.

Kazhdan, Alexander, ed. *The Oxford Dictionary of Byzantium.* 3 vols. New York: Oxford University Press, 1991.

Obolensky, Dimitri. *The Byzantine Commonwealth: Eastern Europe, 500–1453.* London: Weidenfeld and Nicolson, 1971.

Ostrogorsky, George. *History of the Byzantine State.* Revised ed. Oxford: Blackwell, 1969.

Runciman, Steven. *A History of the First Bulgarian Empire.* London: G. Bell & Sons, 1930.

Runciman, Steven. *The Medieval Manichee: A Study of the Christian Dualist Heresy.* Cambridge: Cambridge University Press, 1947.

Shepard, Jonathan. "Emerging Powers in East and Central Europe: The Byzantines, the Bulgarians, and the Rus (800–1200)." In *The New Cambridge Medieval History, Volume II: c.700–c.900*, edited by Rosamond McKitterick, 583–646. Cambridge: Cambridge University Press, 1995.

Stephenson, Paul. *Byzantium's Balkan Frontier: A Political Study of the Northern Balkans, 900–1204.* Cambridge: Cambridge University Press, 2000.

Treadgold, Warren. *A History of the Byzantine State and Society.* Stanford, CA: Stanford University Press, 1997.

Soulis, George C. *The Serbs and Byzantium during the Reign of Tsar Stephen Dušan, 1331–1355, and His Successors.* Washington, D.C.: Dumbarton Oaks, 1984.

Vryonis, Speros. *The Decline of Medieval Hellenism in Asia Minor and the Process of Islamization from the Eleventh through the Fifteenth Century.* Berkeley: University of California Press, 1971.

Zlatarski, Vasil N. *History of the Bulgarian State in the Middle Ages.* Vol. II. Sofia: Science and Art Publishing, 1971.

Ottoman Period

Ágoston, Gábor, and Bruce Masters, eds. *Encyclopedia of the Ottoman Empire.* New York: Facts On File, 2009.

Barkey, Karen. *Empire of Difference: The Ottomans in Comparative Perspective.* Cambridge: Cambridge University Press, 2008.

Braude, Benjamin, and Bernard Lewis, eds. *Christians and Jews in the Ottoman Empire: The Functioning of a Plural Society.* Vol. 1. New York: Holmes & Meier, 1982.

Clayer, Nathalie. "Muslim Brotherhood Networks in the Balkans under Ottoman Rule." In *The Muslim World in the Age of the Crusades*, edited by Carole Hillenbrand, 145–172. Edinburgh: Edinburgh University Press, 2006.

Ćirković, Sima M. *The Serbs*. Oxford: Blackwell Publishing, 2004.

Finkel, Caroline. *Osman's Dream: The History of the Ottoman Empire*. New York: Basic Books, 2005.

Goffman, Daniel. *The Ottoman Empire and Early Modern Europe*. Cambridge: Cambridge University Press, 2002.

Inalcik, Halil. *The Ottoman Empire: The Classical Age, 1300–1600*. Translated by Norman Itzkowitz and Colin Imber. London: Weidenfeld and Nicolson, 1973.

Inalcik, Halil, and Donald Quataert, eds. *An Economic and Social History of the Ottoman Empire, 1300–1914*. Cambridge: Cambridge University Press, 1994.

Jelavich, Barbara. *History of the Balkans: Volume 1, Eighteenth and Nineteenth Centuries*. Cambridge: Cambridge University Press, 1983.

Jelavich, Charles, and Barbara Jelavich. *The Establishment of the Balkan National States, 1804–1920*. Seattle: University of Washington Press, 1977.

Kiel, Machiel. *Ottoman Architecture in Albania, 1385–1912*. Istanbul: Research Centre for Islamic History, Art and Culture (IRCICA), 1990.

Kitromilides, Paschalis M. *Enlightenment and Revolution: The Making of Modern Greece*. Cambridge, MA: Harvard University Press, 2013.

Setton, Kenneth M., ed. *A History of the Crusades: Volume II, The Later Crusades, 1189–1311*. Madison: University of Wisconsin Press, 1969.

Stavrianos, L. S. *The Balkans since 1453*. New York: Holt, Rinehart and Winston, 1965.

Stoianovich, Traian. *Balkan Worlds: The First and Last Europe*. Armonk, NY: M.E. Sharpe, 1994.

Sugar, Peter F. *Southeastern Europe under Ottoman Rule, 1354–1804*. Seattle: University of Washington Press, 1977.

Modern Balkans and Nationalism

Balkelis, Tomas. *The Making of Modern Lithuania*. London: Routledge, 2009.

Banac, Ivo. *The National Question in Yugoslavia: Origins, History, Politics*. Ithaca: Cornell University Press, 1984.

Berend, Ivan T. *History Derailed: Central and Eastern Europe in the Long Nineteenth Century*. Berkeley: University of California Press, 2003.

Clark, Christopher. *The Sleepwalkers: How Europe Went to War in 1914*. New York: Harper, 2013.

Cornwall, Mark. *The Undermining of Austria-Hungary: The Battle for Hearts and Minds*. New York: Palgrave Macmillan, 2000.

Crampton, R. J. *A Concise History of Bulgaria*. 2nd ed. Cambridge: Cambridge University Press, 2005.

Ćirković, Sima M. *The Serbs*. Oxford: Blackwell Publishing, 2004.

Daskalov, Roumen. *The Making of a Nation in the Balkans: Historiography of the Bulgarian Revival*. Budapest: Central European University Press, 2004.

Gallant, Thomas W. *Modern Greece*. London: Arnold, 2001.

Gallant, Thomas W. *Modern Greece: From the War of Independence to the Present*. London: Bloomsbury Academic, 2016.

Hall, Richard C. *The Balkan Wars 1912–1913: Prelude to the First World War*. London: Routledge, 2000.

Hall, Richard C. *The Modern Balkans: A Concise History*. London: Bloomsbury Academic, 2019.

Karakasidou, Anastasia N. *Fields of Wheat, Hills of Blood: Passages to Nationhood in Greek Macedonia, 1870–1990*. Chicago: University of Chicago Press, 1997.

Mazower, Mark. *The Balkans: A Short History*. New York: Modern Library, 2000.

Norris, H. T. *Islam in the Balkans: Religion and Society Between Europe and the Arab World*. Columbia: University of South Carolina Press, 1993.

Roudometof, Victor. *Nationalism, Globalisation, and Orthodoxy: The Social Origins of Ethnic Conflict in the Balkans*. Westport, CT: Greenwood Press, 2001.

Seton-Watson, R. W. *The Rise of Nationality in the Balkans*. London: Constable & Co., 1917.

Sugar, Peter F. *Eastern European Nationalism in the Twentieth Century*. Washington, DC: American University Press, 1995.

Todorova, Maria. *Imagining the Balkans*. Oxford: Oxford University Press, 1997.

Treadway, John D. *The Falcon and the Eagle: Montenegro and Austria-Hungary, 1908–1914*. West Lafayette: Purdue University Press, 1983.

Yugoslavia

Banac, Ivo. *With Stalin Against Tito: Cominformist Splits in Yugoslav Communism*. Ithaca: Cornell University Press, 1988.

Barany, Zoltan. *Democratic Breakdown and the Decline of the Russian Military*. Princeton: Princeton University Press, 2007.

Bieber, Florian. *The Rise of Authoritarianism in the Western Balkans*. Cham: Palgrave Macmillan, 2020.

Burg, Steven L., and Paul S. Shoup. *The War in Bosnia-Herzegovina: Ethnic Conflict and International Intervention*. Armonk, NY: M.E. Sharpe, 1999.

Clark, Mark. *The Death of the Yugoslav Army: 1944–1945*. London: Routledge, 2015.

Cohen, Lenard J. *Broken Bonds: Yugoslavia's Disintegration and Balkan Politics in Transition*. 2nd ed. Boulder: Westview Press, 1995.

Glenny, Misha. *The Fall of Yugoslavia: The Third Balkan War*. Revised ed. London: Penguin Books, 1996.

Gow, James. *Triumph of the Lack of Will: International Diplomacy and the Yugoslav War*. London:

Wider Eastern Europe

Bartov, Omer, and Phyllis Mack, eds. *In God's Name: Genocide and Religion in the Twentieth Century*. New York: Berghahn Books, 2001.

Browning, Christopher R. *Ordinary Men: Reserve Police Battalion 101 and the Final Solution in Poland*. New York: Harper Perennial, 1993.

Deletant, Dennis. *Ceaușescu and the Securitate: Coercion and Dissent in Romania, 1965–1989*. London: Hurst, 1995.

Feinberg, Melissa. *Elusive Equality: Gender, Citizenship, and the Limits of Democracy in Czechoslovakia, 1918–1950*. Pittsburgh: University of Pittsburgh Press, 2006.

Gellner, Ernest. *Nations and Nationalism*. Ithaca: Cornell University Press, 1983.

Kallis, Aristotle A. *Genocide and Fascism: The Eliminationist Drive in Fascist Europe*. London: Routledge, 2009.

Kramer, Mark. "The Collapse of East European Communism and the Repercussions within the Soviet Union." *Journal of Cold War Studies* 5, no. 4 (2003): 178–256.

Mazower, Mark. *Inside Hitler's Greece: The Experience of Occupation, 1941–44*. New Haven: Yale University Press, 1993.

Mazower, Mark. *Salonica, City of Ghosts: Christians, Muslims and Jews, 1430–1950*. New York: Vintage, 2006.

Rothschild, Joseph. *East Central Europe Between the Two World Wars*. Seattle: University of Washington Press, 1974.

Rothschild, Joseph, and Nancy M. Wingfield. *Return to Diversity: A Political History of East Central Europe Since World War II*. 4th ed. New York: Oxford University Press, 2008.

Seton-Watson, Hugh. *Eastern Europe Between the Wars, 1918–1941*. Cambridge: Cambridge University Press, 1945.

Tismaneanu, Vladimir. *Stalinism for All Seasons: A Political History of Romanian Communism.* Berkeley: University of California Press, 2003.

Trybuś, Magdalena. *The Holocaust in Southeastern Europe: Historiography, Archives, and Sources.* Warsaw: Polish Academy of Sciences, 2015.

Zubok, Vladislav. *A Failed Empire: The Soviet Union in the Cold War from Stalin to Gorbachev.* Chapel Hill: University of North Carolina Press, 2007.

Zürcher, Erik J. *Turkey: A Modern History.* London: I.B. Tauris, 2004.

Salads and Sharing's

Shopska Salad

Ingredients: (2-3 servings)

- 1 large cucumber
- 2-3 middle-size beef tomatoes
- 1 green pepper
- 1 middle-size onion
- 1 bunch of parsley
- 150gr. Of Feta cheese
- Olive oil, salt and wine vinegar

Instructions:

- Chop the cucumber, the tomatoes, and the pepper into squares and place it in a bowl.
- Then, add the finely chopped onion and parsley.
- Mixed all together with the olive oil, salt, and wine vinegar on your test.
- Then spread the Feta cheese on top.

Snowhite, Tzatziki

Ingredients:

- 2 cucumbers
- 500gr. Yoghurt
- Total brand or 10% fat one
- Fresh bunch of dill
- 2-3 cloves of garlic
- Olive oil and salt
- Walnuts finely chopped

Preparation:

- Place the yoghurt in a bowl and mix well.
- Cut the cucumbers into the smallest squares you can and add it to the yoghurt.
- Chop or mince the garlic, and finely chop the dill.
- Add all ingredients in the bowl and mix well, adding olive and salt to your taste.
- The original recipe is with walnuts.

Russian Salad

Ingredients:

- 1kg of potatoes, any size and type
- 2 middle carrots
- 1 pack of ham, any
- 1 jar of gherkins
- 1 can of garden peas
- 1 large jar of mayonnaise

Instructions:

- Boil the potatoes, peel it, and cut it into small squares.
- Boil the carrots, cut it, and add it to the potatoes.
- Place it in a bowl, add the peas.
- Cut the gherkins and the ham into a small square and add it to the bowl.
- Mix all ingredients well and add the mayonnaise. Mix well.
- Add some salt if need it.
- Leave it in the fridge for a few hours before serving.

Yoghurt with Pepper

Ingredients:

- 3-4 red baked peppers
- 200gr. Of Feta cheese
- 500gr. Of Yoghurt, the thickest you can find
- 1-2 cloves of garlic
- Dill, salt and olive oil

Instructions:

- Place the Yoghurt in a bowl and mix it well.
- Then crumble the feta cheese.
- Cut the pepper, you can bake it yourself or buy a jar of it, but be careful not to have vinegar in it.
- Add the garlic and the dill, finely chopped. Add salt and olive oil to your test.

Tubule

Ingredients:

- 1 cube vegetable stock
- 150gr. Of bulgur wheat
- 2 large tomatoes
- One bag of parsley

Instructions:

- Place the vegetable stock in 400 ml. of water and place it on the hob.
- When the water boils, add the bulgur and stir quickly for a few minutes.
- Then remove it from the hob and cover with the lid. Leave it for 20 minutes. Stir once midway.
- Chop the tomatoes into a very small cubes and add it to the bulgur.
- Add the parsley, very finely chopped.
- Add salt if necessary.

Romanian Salad

Ingredients:

- 1kg. of potatoes
- 5-6 gherkins
- 1 leak
- One bag of parsley
- 2 eggs
- Green olives
- Salt and olive oil

Instructions:

- Boil the potatoes and the eggs (hard-boil)
- Peel the potatoes and cut it into mid-size cubes, and place it in a bowl.
- Peel and cut the eggs and add it to the potatoes.
- Cut the gherkins and the leek finely and add it to the bowl.
- Mix all ingredients well and test it with salt and olive oil.

Courgettes with Yoghurt Dip

Ingredients:

- 3-4 courgettes
- Salt and olive oil for frying
- For the dip:
- One yoghurt, any
- Dill, salt, and garlic

Instructions:

- Cut the courgettes into 1-2 cm circles and fry it till golden
- Mix the yoghurt with the finely chopped dill and garlic
- Lay one-layer of courgettes and one from the yoghurt dip

Fried Aubergine

Ingredients:

- 3 aubergines
- One lemon
- 2 cloves of garlic
- Salt and olive oil

Instructions:

- Cut the aubergines into one to two cm circles and fry it.
- For a healthier option, brush the aubergines with olive oil and bake it
- In a bowl, squeeze the lemon, add finely chopped garlic and some parsley
- Place the fried aubergine on a plate and brush it with the lemon mix.

Pepper and Aubergine Meze

Ingredients:

- 1 big aubergine
- 2 red Romano pepper
- 1 medium white onion
- 2 cloves of garlic
- Parsley
- One lemon
- Salt and olive oil

Instructions:

- Piers the aubergine with a fork, put some salt and a bit of olive oil, cover it with foil, and bake it for around 30 minutes.
- Do the same with the pepper.
- Leave it for a few minutes and peel it, then cut it finely.
- Add finely chopped garlic, onion and parsley. Squeeze the lemon and add it.
- Sall on your test.

Soups And Stews

Chicken Soup

Ingredients:

- 2 medium potatoes, diced
- 1 large carrot, diced
- 1 small onion, diced
- 1 green pepper, diced
- 1 chicken breast or thighs cut into bite-sized pieces
- 1 litre of water
- 1 chicken stock cube
- 1/3 cup fide (short, thin pasta or vermicelli)
- 1 egg
- 2–3 tablespoons plain yoghurt
- Salt and pepper to taste

Instructions:

1. Prepare the broth:

   - In a large pot, bring 1 litre of water to a boil.
   - Add the chicken stock cube and stir until dissolved.

2. Add ingredients:

   - Once the water is boiling, add the diced potatoes, carrots, onion, green pepper, and chicken pieces.

3. Cook:

   - Let everything simmer until the vegetables and chicken are fully cooked, about 20–25 minutes.

4. Add pasta:

   - Stir in the fide (or vermicelli) and cook for another 5–7 minutes, or until the pasta is tender.

5. Prepare egg mixture:

   - In a small bowl, whisk the egg together with the yoghurt until smooth.

6. Temper and add to soup:

   - Let the soup cool slightly until it's warm but not hot.
   - Slowly add a ladle of warm soup into the egg- yoghurt mixture, stirring constantly to temper it.
   - Then, slowly pour the mixture back into the soup pot, stirring continuously.

7. Finish cooking:

- Return the soup to a gentle boil and cook for another 5 minutes. Season with salt and pepper to taste.

Serving Suggestion:

- Serve warm with fresh bread or croutons if desired.

Meatballs soup

Ingredients:

- For the meatballs:
- 300g ground beef or mixed ground meat (beef and pork)
- 1 small onion, finely grated or minced
- 2 tablespoons uncooked rice
- 1 egg
- Salt and pepper to taste
- Optional: 1 tablespoon chopped parsley

For the soup:

- 1 large carrot, diced
- 1 medium potato, diced
- 1 small onion, chopped
- 1 green pepper, diced
- 1 tablespoon oil
- 1.5 litres of water
- 1 chicken or vegetable stock cube
- Salt and pepper to taste
- Optional: a handful of fide (vermicelli) or small pasta

For finishing:

- 1 egg
- 2–3 tablespoons plain yoghurt or sour cream

Instructions:

1. Make the meatballs:

- In a bowl, mix the ground meat with grated onion, rice, egg, salt, pepper, and parsley.
- Shape into small balls (about the size of a walnut) and set aside.

2. Prepare the base:

- In a large pot, heat a tablespoon of oil.
- Add the chopped onion, carrot, potato, and green pepper. Sauté for 2–3 minutes.

3. Add water and stock:

- Pour in 1.5 litres of water and add the stock cube. Bring to a boil.

4. Add meatballs:

- Once boiling, gently add the meatballs one by one into the soup.
- Lower the heat to a simmer and cook for about 20–25 minutes, until the meatballs and rice inside are cooked through.

5. Add pasta (optional):

- If using fide or pasta, add it in the last 7–10 minutes of cooking.

6. Prepare egg mixture:

- In a bowl, whisk the egg with the yoghurt (or sour cream) until smooth.

7. Temper and mix in:

- When the soup is warm but not boiling hot, add a ladle of soup into the egg yoghurt mix, stir, and then slowly add the mixture back into the pot while stirring.

8. Final simmer:

- Let the soup simmer gently for another 5 minutes. Do not boil hard after adding the egg mixture.

Serving Suggestion:

- Season to taste and serve warm with bread.

Lentil Stew

Ingredients:

- 1 cup brown or green lentils (rinsed)
- 1 medium onion, chopped
- 1 medium carrot, diced
- 1–2 cloves garlic, minced
- 1 small green pepper (optional), diced
- 2 tablespoons tomato paste or 1 grated fresh tomato
- 2–3 tablespoons sunflower oil (or vegetable oil)
- 1 teaspoon paprika (Bulgarian sweet paprika)
- 1 teaspoon dried savoury (чубрица / chubritsa)
- 1 bay leaf
- Salt and pepper to taste
- 4 cups (1 litre) water
- Optional: a splash of vinegar before serving

Instructions:

1. Sauté vegetables:

   - In a pot, heat the oil.
   - Add the chopped onion, carrot, and green pepper (if using).
   - Sauté for 4–5 minutes until softened.

2. Add paprika and garlic:

   - Stir in the paprika and minced garlic.
   - Cook for 30 seconds to release the aroma, but don't let it burn.

3. Add tomato paste and lentils:

   - Add the tomato paste (or grated tomato), stir for 1–2 minutes, then add the rinsed lentils.
   - Mix well to coat.

4. Pour water and season:

   - Add 4 cups of water, a bay leaf, and a pinch of salt.
   - Bring to a boil, then reduce the heat to low.

5. Simmer:

   - Cover and simmer for about 35–40 minutes or until the lentils are tender.
   - Stir occasionally and add more water if it gets too thick.

6. Season and finish:

- Add savoury, pepper, and more salt to taste.
- Simmer for another 5 minutes. Remove the bay leaf before serving.

7. Optional touch:

- Add a splash of vinegar right before serving for a traditional Bulgarian flavour.

Serving suggestion:

- Serve warm with crusty bread or white rice on the side. This dish is often enjoyed with a side of pickled vegetables or fresh salad.

Cold soup-Tarator

Ingredients:

- 2 cups (400–500g) plain yoghurt (preferably Bulgarian-style, but Greek works too)
- 1 cucumber (peeled and finely chopped or grated)
- 1–2 cloves garlic, minced
- 2 tablespoons chopped fresh dill
- 1–2 tablespoons sunflower oil or olive oil
- 1/2 teaspoon salt (or to taste)
- 1 cup cold water (adjust for desired thickness)
- Optional: crushed walnuts for garnish

Instructions:

1. Prepare the cucumber:

- Peel the cucumber and chop it into small cubes or grate it, depending on your preference.

2. Mix the yoghurt :

- In a bowl, whisk the yoghurt until smooth.
- Add cold water gradually and mix until you reach a soup-like consistency.

3. Add ingredients:

- Stir in the cucumber, minced garlic, chopped dill, salt, and oil.

4. Chill:

- Refrigerate the tarator for at least 30 minutes to let the flavours combine, and serve it cold.

Serving Suggestion:

- Serve chilled, optionally topped with crushed walnuts and a drizzle of extra oil.

Aubergine Stew

Ingredients:

- 2–3 medium aubergines (eggplants)
- 4–5 ripe tomatoes (or 1 can of chopped tomatoes)
- 1 onion, finely chopped
- 3–4 cloves garlic, minced
- 1–2 green peppers (optional), chopped
- 3–4 tablespoons sunflower oil (or olive oil)
- 1 teaspoon sugar (optional, to balance tomato acidity)
- Salt and pepper to taste
- 1 tablespoon chopped parsley (for garnish)

Instructions:

1. Prepare the aubergines:

- Wash and slice the aubergines into rounds or cubes.
- Sprinkle with salt and let them sit for 20–30 minutes to remove bitterness.
- Rinse and pat dry.

2. Fry or bake aubergines:

- In a pan, fry the aubergine slices in oil until golden and soft, or roast them in the oven at 200°C (390°F) for about 25 minutes, flipping halfway.

3. Prepare the sauce:

- In another pan, heat a bit of oil and sauté the onion and green pepper (if using) until soft.
- Add the minced garlic, stir briefly, then add the chopped tomatoes.
- Simmer for 10–15 minutes until the sauce thickens.
- Add salt, pepper, and a pinch of sugar if needed.

4. Combine:

- Arrange the cooked aubergines in a baking dish or wide pan.
- Pour the tomato sauce over them and simmer together on low heat for 10 more minutes, or bake in the oven for 15 minutes to melt the flavours.

Serving Suggestion:

- Garnish with chopped parsley. Serve warm with bread or cold as a mezze or side dish.

Beans and Sausage Stew

Ingredients:

- 2 cups (400g) dry white beans (or 2 cans of cooked beans)
- 1–2 smoked sausages (lukanka, sujuk, or any smoked/kielbasa-style sausage), sliced
- 1 onion, chopped
- 1 carrot, diced
- 1 green or red pepper, diced
- 3–4 cloves garlic, minced
- 2 tablespoons tomato paste or 1 grated tomato
- 1 teaspoon sweet paprika
- 1–2 bay leaves
- 1 teaspoon dried savoury (chubritsa)
- Salt and black pepper to taste
- 4 tablespoons sunflower oil
- Water as needed

Optional: fresh parsley for garnish

Instructions:

1. Prepare the beans (if using dry):

- Rinse and soak the beans overnight. Drain and boil in fresh water for about 40 minutes or until nearly tender.
- Drain again.

2. Sauté the vegetables:

- In a pan, heat oil and sauté the onion, carrot, and pepper for 5–6 minutes. Add garlic and paprika, stir for 30 seconds, then add tomato paste or grated tomato. Cook for 2 more minutes.

3. Combine in a baking dish:

- In a large clay pot or deep baking dish, combine the beans, sautéed vegetables, and sliced sausage.
- Add bay leaves, savory, salt, and pepper. Pour in hot water just enough to cover the contents.

4. Bake:
- Cover the dish with a lid or foil.
- Bake in a preheated oven at 180°C (350°F) for about 1.5 to 2 hours, or until the beans are soft and the stew is thickened. If using canned beans, reduce baking time to about 45–60 minutes.

5. Uncover for the last 15 min (optional):

- Remove the lid/foil during the last 15–20 minutes of baking for a slightly crispy top.

Serving Suggestion:

- Let it rest for a few minutes before serving. Garnish with parsley if desired.

Meatballs Stew

Ingredients:

For the meatballs:

- 500g ground meat (beef, pork, or a mix)
- 1 small onion, grated or very finely chopped
- 1 slice of bread, soaked in water and squeezed (or 2 tbsp breadcrumbs)
- 1 egg
- 1 tsp cumin (optional but traditional)
- Salt and black pepper to taste
- 1–2 tbsp fresh parsley, chopped
- Sunflower oil for frying

For the tomato stew:

- 2–3 tbsp sunflower oil
- 1 small onion, chopped
- 2–3 cloves garlic, minced
- 400g canned chopped tomatoes or 4–5 ripe tomatoes, grated
- 1 tbsp tomato paste (optional for richer flavour)
- 1 tsp sugar (to balance acidity)
- Salt and pepper to taste
- 1 tsp savoury (chubritsa) or basil (optional)
- 1–2 bay leaves
- 1 cup water or stock

Instructions:

1. Make the meatballs:

    - In a bowl, mix ground meat, onion, soaked bread, egg, parsley, cumin, salt, and pepper. Knead the mixture well and shape into small meatballs.

2. Fry the meatballs:

    - Heat some oil in a pan and lightly fry the meatballs on all sides until browned (they don't need to be fully cooked inside). Set aside.

3. Prepare the tomato sauce:

    - In a pot, heat oil and sauté the chopped onion until soft.
    - Add garlic and stir briefly.
    - Add grated or canned tomatoes, tomato paste, sugar, salt, pepper, bay leaf, and herbs.
    - Pour in water/stock and bring to a simmer.

4. Simmer meatballs in sauce:

    - Add the browned meatballs to the tomato sauce.
    - Cover and simmer gently for about 20–25 minutes, until the meatballs are cooked through and the sauce has thickened.

Finish and serve:

- Remove the bay leaf. Serve hot with mashed potatoes, white rice, or fresh bread.

Mackerel With Beans Stew

Ingredients:

- 2 whole mackerels (cleaned, gutted, and halved or filleted)
- 2 cups cooked white beans (or 1 cup dry beans, soaked and boiled)
- 1 onion, finely chopped
- 1 carrot, diced
- 1 green pepper, chopped
- 2–3 cloves garlic, minced
- 400g canned chopped tomatoes or 4 fresh tomatoes, grated
- 3-4 medium-sized pickle gherkins, not the sweet one
- 1–2 tablespoons tomato paste
- 1 teaspoon sweet paprika
- 1 bay leaf
- 1 teaspoon dried savoury (чубрица/chubritsa)
- Salt and pepper to taste
- 3–4 tablespoons sunflower oil
- Fresh parsley for garnish

Instructions:

1. Cook the beans (if using dry):

- Soak dry beans overnight. Boil in fresh water until tender but not mushy. Drain and set aside.

2. Prepare the sauce:

- In a deep pan, heat oil and sauté onion, carrot, and pepper until soft.
- Add garlic and paprika and stir briefly.
- Add chopped tomatoes, tomato paste, bay leaf, salt, pepper, gherkins and savoury.
- Simmer for 10–15 minutes until slightly thickened.

3. Combine with beans:

- Add the cooked beans to the sauce and stir well.
- Let it simmer for 5 more minutes.
- Taste and adjust seasoning.

4. Assemble and bake:

- In a large baking dish, spread the bean mixture evenly.
- Lay the mackerel fillets or pieces on top.
- Drizzle a little oil over the fish and add a pinch of salt and pepper.

5. Bake:

- Preheat the oven to 180°C (350°F).
- Bake uncovered for 25–30 minutes, or until the fish is cooked through and the top is slightly caramelized.

Serving Suggestion:

- Garnish with chopped parsley and serve hot with fresh bread or salad.

Main Dishes

Chicken Kavarma

Ingredients:

- 500–600g chicken (thighs or breast), cut into bite-sized pieces
- 1 large onion, sliced
- 1–2 green or red peppers, chopped
- 1 carrot, sliced
- 200g mushrooms, sliced (optional)
- 2 tomatoes, grated (or 1/2 cup canned tomatoes)
- 2 cloves garlic, minced
- 100ml white wine
- 2–3 tablespoons sunflower oil
- 1 teaspoon paprika (sweet)
- 1 teaspoon savory (чубрица)
- 1 bay leaf
- Salt and black pepper to taste

Optional: 1–2 tablespoons chopped parsley

Instructions:

1. Sear the chicken:

    - In a large pan, heat the oil and brown the chicken pieces for 3–4 minutes. Remove and set aside.

2. Sauté the vegetables:

    - In the same pan, add a bit more oil if needed and sauté the onions, peppers, carrots, and

mushrooms (if using) until softened.
- Add the garlic and paprika and stir for 30 seconds.

3. Deglaze with wine:

- Return the chicken to the pan. Add the white wine and let it simmer for 2–3 minutes to let the alcohol evaporate.

4. Add tomatoes and seasoning:

- Stir in the grated tomatoes, savoury, bay leaf, salt, and pepper.
- Simmer everything together for about 10 minutes.

5. Bake:

- Transfer everything into a clay pot (gyuveche) or baking dish.
- Cover and bake at 180°C (350°F) for about 30–40 minutes, until the chicken is tender and the sauce has thickened.

Serving Suggestion:

- Sprinkle with fresh parsley before serving. Serve hot with bread, rice, or potatoes.

Musaka

Ingredients:

For the base:

- 500g minced meat (usually pork or a pork-beef mix)
- 1 kg potatoes, peeled and diced into small cubes
- 1 medium onion, chopped
- 1 medium carrot (optional), grated or finely chopped
- 2 tablespoons sunflower oil
- 1 teaspoon paprika
- Salt and pepper to taste
- 1 teaspoon savory (чубрица)
- 1–2 tomatoes, grated (or 1/2 cup canned tomatoes)
- 1/2 cup water

For the topping:

- 2 eggs
- 1 cup plain yoghurt
- 2 tablespoons flour
- Salt to taste

Instructions:

1. Cook the filling:

   - In a large pan, heat oil and sauté the onion and carrot until soft.
   - Add the minced meat and cook until browned.
   - Add paprika, salt, pepper, savoury, and grated tomato.
   - Cook for 5 more minutes, then stir in the diced potatoes and water.

2. Bake the base:

   - Pour the mixture into a greased baking dish and spread evenly.
   - Bake in a preheated oven at 180°C (350°F) for about 40–45 minutes, or until the potatoes are soft and the liquid is mostly absorbed.

3. Prepare the topping:

   - In a bowl, whisk the eggs with the yoghurt, flour, and a pinch of salt until smooth.

4. Add topping and finish baking:

   - Pour the egg mixture evenly over the baked base.

- Return to the oven and bake for another 15–20 minutes or until the topping is golden and set.

Rest and serve:

- Let the moussaka sit for 10–15 minutes before serving so it sets properly.
- Cut into squares and serve warm, often with a dollop of yoghurt or a fresh salad.

Yoghurt Eggs

Ingredients:

- 4 eggs
- 1 cup plain yoghurt (preferably Bulgarian-style or Greek)
- 2 cloves garlic, minced or crushed
- Salt to taste
- 1 tablespoon vinegar (for poaching)
- 2 tablespoons butter
- 1 teaspoon sweet paprika

Instructions:

1. Prepare the yoghurt base:
   - In a bowl, mix the yoghurt with crushed garlic and a pinch of salt.
   - Set aside at room temperature.

2. Poach the eggs:

   - Fill a pot with water and bring it to a gentle simmer.
   - Add 1 tablespoon of vinegar.
   - Crack each egg into a small bowl, then gently slide it into the simmering water.
   - Poach for 2–3 minutes until the whites are set, but the yolks remain runny.
   - Remove with a slotted spoon and drain on a paper towel.

3. Prepare the paprika butter:

- In a small pan, melt the butter.
- Once it starts to foam, add the paprika and stir for a few seconds until fragrant. Remove from heat.

4. Assemble:

- Spread the garlic yoghurt on a serving plate.
- Place the poached eggs on top.
- Drizzle with the hot paprika butter.

Serving Suggestion:

Serve immediately with crusty bread.

Tip: For extra richness, you can sprinkle a bit of crumbled feta (sirene) over the eggs before adding the paprika butter.

Wine Kebab

Ingredients:

- 600g pork (shoulder or leg), cut into bite-sized cubes
- 1 large onion, chopped
- 3–4 tablespoons sunflower oil
- 2 tablespoons flour
- 1 tablespoon tomato paste
- 1 teaspoon sweet paprika
- 200ml dry red wine
- 1–2 bay leaves
- 1 teaspoon savoury (чубрица, optional)
- Salt and pepper to taste
- 2 cups water or stock

For serving:

- Cooked white rice or mashed potatoes

Optional: chopped parsley for garnish

Instructions:

1. Sear the meat:

    - In a large pot, heat the oil.
    - Add the pork and brown on all sides.
    - Remove and set aside.

2. Sauté onions:

    - In the same pot, add the chopped onion and cook until golden and soft.

3. Add flour and paprika:

    - Sprinkle in the flour and stir well until it absorbs the oil and starts to brown slightly.
    - Add the paprika and stir quickly (don't let it burn).

4. Deglaze and simmer:

    - Add the tomato paste and pour in the wine.
    - Stir, scraping the bottom of the pan, then return the meat to the pot.

5. Add water and season:

    - Add enough water or stock to cover the meat.
    - Add bay leaves, savoury, salt, and pepper.

- Bring to a boil, then reduce heat to low.

6. Cook:

- Simmer uncovered or partially covered for about 1 to 1.5 hours until the meat is tender and the sauce thickens. Add more water if needed.

Serving Suggestion:

- Spoon the wine kebab over rice or mashed potatoes and garnish with chopped parsley if desired.

Tip: This dish tastes even better the next day as the flavours deepen.

Chicken Potatoes

Ingredients:

- 4-6 chicken pieces (drumsticks, thighs, or a whole cut-up chicken)
- 1 kg (2.2 lbs) potatoes, peeled and cut into chunks
- 1 large onion, sliced (optional)
- 3–4 garlic cloves, whole or chopped
- 1 teaspoon sweet paprika
- 1 teaspoon dried savoury (чубрица) or thyme
- Salt and black pepper to taste
- 4 tablespoons sunflower oil (or olive oil)
- 1/2 cup water or chicken stock
- Optional: 1 tomato, grated or 1 tbsp tomato paste

Instructions:

Preheat the oven:

- Set your oven to 200°C (390°F).

Prepare the potatoes:

- In a large baking dish, toss the potatoes with sliced onion, garlic, paprika, savoury, salt, pepper, and 2 tablespoons of oil.

Add chicken:

- Season the chicken pieces with salt, pepper, and a bit more paprika. Place them on top of the potatoes. Drizzle with the remaining oil.

Add liquid:

- Pour about 1/2 cup of water or chicken stock into the dish to help everything cook and stay moist. If using tomato paste or grated tomato, mix it into the liquid before adding.

Bake:

- Cover with foil and bake for 40 minutes. Then uncover and bake for another 30–40 minutes, or until the chicken is golden and the potatoes are tender. Baste occasionally with the pan juices.

Serving Suggestion:

Serve hot, often with a simple salad or pickled vegetables.

Kapama

Ingredients:

- Meats (you can adjust by taste or availability):
- 500g pork (shoulder or ribs), cut in chunks
- 500g chicken legs or thighs (bone-in, skin-on preferred)
- 300g beef (optional, like brisket or stew meat)
- 2–3 sausages (Bulgarian lukanka or blood sausage if authentic; or chorizo/kielbasa as substitute)

Others:

- 1 small head of sour cabbage (sauerkraut) — chopped + a few whole leaves
- 1 cup rice (short- or medium-grain)
- 2 medium onions, finely chopped
- 2–3 tbsp vegetable oil or lard
- 1 cup dry red wine
- 1 tsp sweet paprika
- 1 tsp black pepper
- 1 tsp salt (adjust depending on how salty your sauerkraut is)
- 2–3 bay leaves
- 4–5 allspice berries or cloves (optional but traditional)
- 1 tsp thyme (optional)

Instructions:

1. Preheat Oven

    - Set oven to 150°C (300°F) for slow cooking.

2. Sauté Onions & Rice

    - In a pan, heat oil or lard.

- Sauté onions until soft.
- Add rice and stir for 2–3 minutes until lightly toasted.
- Season with paprika, salt, pepper. Set aside.

3. Sear the Meats (Optional but Recommended)

- Quickly brown the pork and beef pieces in the same pan. This adds flavour.
- Chicken can go in raw, but you may brown it too if preferred.

4. Layer the Kapama

- In a large clay pot (gyuvetch) or heavy oven-safe pot with a lid:
- Start with a layer of chopped sauerkraut.
- Add a layer of rice-onion mixture.
- Then a layer of meat
- Repeat layers until all ingredients are used up.
- Top with whole sauerkraut leaves to seal the contents.

5. Add Wine & Seasonings

- Pour the red wine evenly over the top.
- Add a splash of water if needed to just barely cover the bottom (don't flood it).
- Add bay leaves and allspice between layers or on top.

6. Cover & Bake

- Cover with a tight lid or seal with aluminium foil and a dough edge for steam-tightness.
- Bake for 4–6 hours at 150°C (300°F). No stirring!
- You can go lower (120–130°C) and cook overnight — traditional!

Serving

- Let it rest for 15–20 minutes before serving.
- Serve straight from the pot with crusty bread and a glass of red wine.
- Leftovers are even better the next day.

Rise with Tomatoes and Kalamata Olives

Ingredients:

- 1 cup rice (short- or medium-grain preferred, like Arborio or round grain)
- 1 medium onion, finely chopped
- 2–3 tbsp sunflower oil or olive oil
- 2 cups fresh tomatoes, peeled and chopped
- (or 1 can diced tomatoes – about 400g)
- 1 cup of Kalamata olives, with or without stones
- 2 ½ cups hot water or vegetable broth
- 1 tsp paprika
- Salt and black pepper to taste
- 1 tsp sugar (optional, balances the acidity of tomatoes)
- 1 tbsp chopped parsley (for garnish)

Instructions:

1. Sauté the Onion

In a wide pot or deep skillet, heat the oil.
Add the chopped onion and cook until soft and translucent (about 5–6 minutes).

2. Add Rice and Paprika

- Stir in the rice and cook for 1–2 minutes until slightly glossy.
- Add the paprika and stir well — this gives it color and flavor.

3. Add Tomatoes

- Add the chopped tomatoes (or canned tomatoes).
- Cook for 5 minutes, stirring occasionally, until tomatoes start to break down and thicken.
- Add the Kalamata olives.

4. Add Water/Broth

- Pour in the hot water or broth. Add salt, pepper, and a pinch of sugar if needed.
- Bring to a boil, then reduce the heat to low.
- Cover and simmer gently for 15–20 minutes, or until the rice is cooked and has absorbed the liquid.
- Stir occasionally to prevent sticking.

5. Rest and Serve

- Turn off the heat and let the rice rest, covered, for 10 minutes.
- Fluff with a fork and garnish with fresh parsley.

Serbian Tatar Köfte

Ingredients:

For the Köfte:

- 500g ground beef (or a mix of beef and lamb)
- 1 small onion, grated or finely minced
- 2 cloves garlic, minced
- 1 slice of bread, soaked in water or milk, then squeezed and crumbled
- 1 egg
- 1 tbsp parsley, finely chopped
- 1 tsp paprika
- ½ tsp ground cumin
- ½ tsp black pepper
- Salt to taste (about 1 tsp)

Optional: pinch of chilli flakes

For the filling:

- 3-4 pickle gherkins, not the sweet ones
- 100-150 g hard cheese, like cheddar

Instructions:

1. Prepare the Meat Mixture

    - In a large bowl, combine the ground meat, grated onion, garlic, soaked bread, egg, parsley, and all spices.
    - Mix thoroughly by hand until well combined.
    - Let it rest for 15–20 minutes in the fridge for better binding.

2. Shape the Köfte

    - With wet hands, form the mixture into oval or round patties (about palm-sized, 1.5 cm thick). Make two of these for every Kofte.
    - Cut the gherkins and the cheese into a short line to fit inside the round patties.
    - Between every two round meet patties, place some of the gherkins and the cheese.
    - Stick the edges of the kofte very well.

3. Cooking:

    - You can grill it, fry it or bake it

Pilav With Chicken

Ingredients:

For the chicken:

- 500–700g chicken (bone-in thighs, drumsticks, or a whole breast)
- Salt to taste
- 1 small onion, halved
- 1 bay leaf (optional)
- 5–6 cups water (to make broth)

For the rice:

- 2 cups baldo rice or long-grain rice (basmati also works)
- 2 tbsp butter (or a mix of butter and olive oil)
- 1 tbsp oil
- 1 tsp salt
- 1 tsp sugar (optional – traditional for balance)
- ½ cup chickpeas (optional; canned or pre-cooked)
- 3 cups chicken broth (from boiling the chicken)

Instructions:

1. Cook the Chicken & Make Broth

- In a pot, add chicken, onion, bay leaf, salt, and water.

- Boil and simmer for 25–30 minutes until chicken is tender.
- Remove chicken, shred or cut into pieces. Set aside.
- Strain and reserve 3 cups of the broth.

2. Wash & Soak the Rice

- Rinse the rice in cold water 2–3 times until the water runs clear.
- Soak in warm water for 15–20 minutes. Drain well before cooking.

3. Cook the Pilav

- In a wide pot, melt butter and oil over medium heat.
- Add the drained rice and toast for 4–5 minutes, stirring constantly until slightly translucent.
- Add chickpeas (if using).
- Pour in 3 cups of hot chicken broth.
- Add the chicken
- Add salt and sugar.
- Bring to a boil, then reduce the heat to low.
- Cover and simmer for 12–15 minutes, or until the liquid is absorbed.

4. Steam & Finish

- Turn off the heat and let the pilav rest covered for 10 minutes.
- Fluff gently with a fork.

Albanian Lamb Dish

Ingredients:

For the filling:

- 500g lamb liver and meat, finely chopped
- 1 medium onion, finely chopped
- 1 cup rice, rinsed (Ambrosio is best)
- 1 bunch green onions, chopped
- 1 bunch fresh parsley, chopped
- 1 bunch fresh mint, chopped
- 1 small tomato, finely chopped (optional)
- 1 tablespoon sunflower oil or olive oil
- 1 teaspoon salt
- 1 teaspoon black pepper
- 1 teaspoon paprika
- 500ml water or broth
- For the topping:
- 2 large eggs
- 200g plain yoghurt
- A pinch of baking soda
- Salt and pepper to taste

Instructions:

1. Prepare the Filling:

    - In a large skillet or casserole, heat the oil over medium heat
    - Add the chopped onion and sauté until translucent.
    - Add the chopped lamb liver and meat and cook until browned.
    - Stir in the rice, green onions, parsley, mint, and tomato (if using).
    - Season with salt, pepper, and paprika.
    - Add the water or broth and simmer until the rice is partially cooked and the liquid is absorbed.
    - Remove from heat and let the mixture cool.
    - Preheat your oven to 180°C (350°F)

2. Prepare the Topping:

    - In a bowl, whisk together the eggs, yoghurt, baking soda, salt, and pepper until smooth.
    - Pour the topping evenly over the rise and meat mixture.

3. Bake:

    - Cover the baking dish with the lid or aluminium foil and bake for 40 minutes.
    - Remove the foil and bake for an additional 20 minutes, or until the top is golden brown and set.

Desserts

Croissant Cake

Ingredients:

- 6 plain croissants (preferably a day or two old)
- Or chocolate, any filled croissant
- 1 litre (4.2 cups) milk
- 200g (1 cup) sugar
- 5 large eggs
- 2 teaspoons vanilla extract

Instructions:

1. Prepare the Croissants:

    - Slice each croissant into 2–3 rings, depending on their size.
    - In a round cake pan 20–22 cm (8–9 inch) or a similar-sized baking dish, spread some of the sugar and bake it in the oven till the sugar melts.
    - Alternatively, you can melt sugar separately and cover the base of the pan
    - Arrange the croissant rings, sticked to the base of the cake pan

2. Make the Custard:

    - In a mixing bowl, whisk together the milk, sugar, eggs, and vanilla extract until well combined.

3. Assemble the Cake:

    - Pour the custard mixture evenly over the arranged croissant rings, ensuring they are well-soaked.
    - Press down gently to submerge the croissants and allow them to absorb the custard.

4. Bake:

    - Preheat your oven to 170°C (340°F).
    - Place the cake pan in the oven and bake for 30–40 minutes, or until the custard is set and the top is golden brown.

5. Cool and Serve:

- Allow the cake to cool to room temperature, then refrigerate for at least 4 hours, preferably overnight, to let the flavours meld.
- Serve chilled.

Baklava With Walnuts

Ingredients:

For the Baklava:

- 400g phyllo dough (about 20 sheets, thawed if frozen)
- 300g walnuts, finely chopped (or mixed with a little ground almond if you like)
- 2 tsp cinnamon (optional)
- 200g unsalted butter, melted
- For the Syrup:
- 300g (1.5 cups) sugar
- 200ml (about ¾ cup) water
- 2 tbsp honey
- Juice of ½ lemon

Optional: 1 clove or a pinch of cinnamon

Instructions:

1. Prepare Filling

   - Finely chop or grind the walnuts.
   - Mix with cinnamon (if using).

2. Prepare Pan and Dough

   - Preheat oven to 170°C (340°F).
   - Brush the bottom and sides of a 9x13-inch (23x33 cm) baking dish with melted butter.
   - Place a sheet of phyllo in the dish. Brush with butter.
   - Repeat this process with 6–8 sheets to form the base.

3. Add Filling Layers

   - Sprinkle ⅓ of the walnut mixture evenly.
   - Cover with 3–4 more phyllo sheets (buttering each).
   - Add another ⅓ of the walnut mixture.
   - Repeat layering until walnuts are used up, finishing with 6–8 phyllo sheets on top (all buttered).

4. Cut Before Baking

   - Using a sharp knife, cut into diamonds or squares all the way to the bottom.
   - This allows the syrup to soak in later.

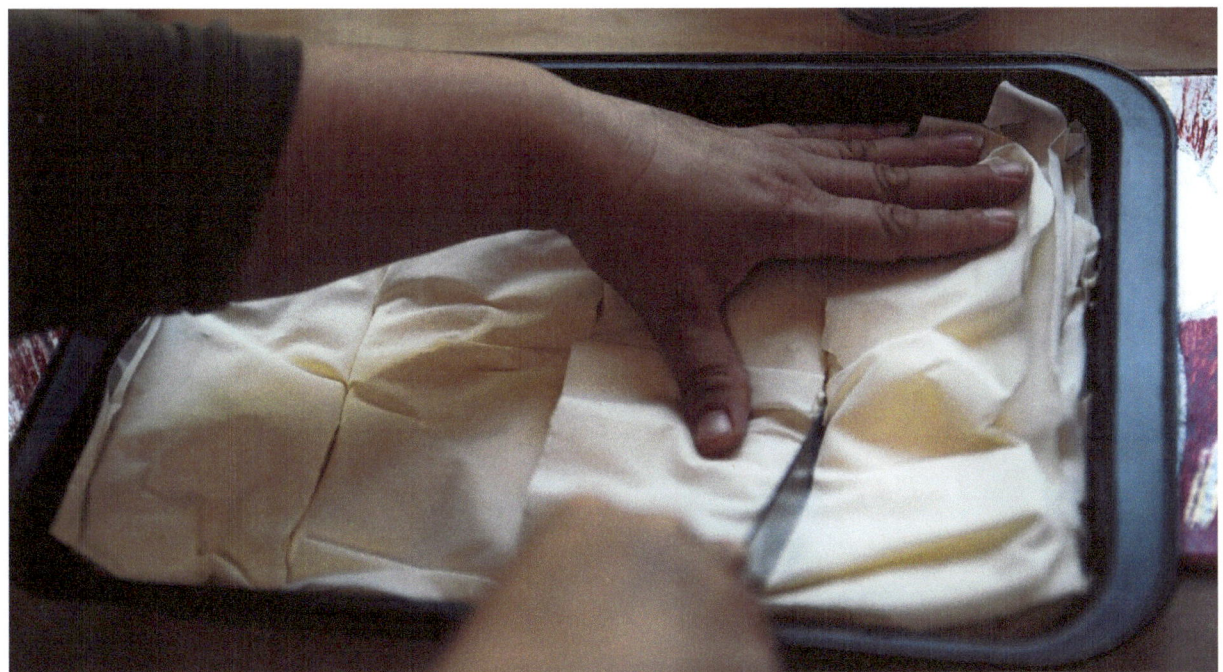

5. Bake

- Bake for 45–50 minutes, until golden and crisp.

6. Make the Syrup

- While baklava bakes, boil sugar, water, lemon juice, and honey for 10–12 minutes.
- Let cool slightly (not ice cold).

7. Add Syrup

- When baklava is hot and just out of the oven, slowly pour cooled syrup over it.
- It will sizzle — that's a good sign!
- Let it sit uncovered at room temperature for several hours or overnight.

Serving Suggestions:

- Best served at room temperature.
- Keeps for up to a week at room temperature or longer refrigerated (though it may lose crispness).

Galaktoboureko

Ingredients:

For the Custard:

- 1 litre of whole milk
- 150g fine semolina (about 1 cup)
- 200g sugar (about 1 cup)
- 2 tbsp unsalted butter
- 2 large eggs
- 1 tsp vanilla extract or 1 packet vanillin sugar
- Zest of 1 lemon or 1 orange
- For the Phyllo:
- 400g phyllo dough (usually 12–14 sheets)
- 150g unsalted butter, melted (for brushing)
- For the Syrup:
- 300g sugar (1½ cups)
- 200ml water (¾–1 cup)
- Juice of ½ lemon

Optional: A piece of lemon peel or cinnamon stick

Instructions:

1. Prepare the Custard

   - In a saucepan, heat the milk gently.
   - Whisk in semolina and sugar slowly to avoid lumps.
   - Cook over medium heat, stirring constantly, until the custard thickens (like cream of wheat).
   - Remove from heat. Stir in butter, lemon/orange zest, and vanilla.
   - Let cool slightly. Beat the eggs and slowly whisk them into the warm custard (off heat).
   - Set aside to cool a bit more.

2. Assemble the Dessert

   - Preheat oven to 170°C (340°F).
   - Brush a 9×13-inch (or 30×20 cm) baking dish with butter.
   - Layer half the phyllo sheets (6–7), one by one, brushing each with butter and letting them hang over the sides.
   - Pour in the custard and spread evenly.
   - Fold over the overhanging phyllo sheets on top of the custard.
   - Add the remaining phyllo sheets, again brushing each with butter.

Tip: Score the top layers gently with a sharp knife (square or diamond shapes), but don't cut all the way through the custard.

3. Bake

- Bake in the preheated oven for 45–50 minutes, or until the top is golden and crisp.

4. Make the Syrup

- While galaktoboureko is baking, boil sugar, water, lemon juice, and optional peel for 7–10 minutes.
- Remove from heat and let cool to lukewarm.

5. Add Syrup

- When the galaktoboureko is hot from the oven, slowly pour the cool syrup over it.
- Let it soak and set for at least 2 hours before serving.

Serving Suggestions:

- Serve at room temperature or chilled.
- Store in the refrigerator for up to 4–5 days.

Revane, Syrup Cake

Ingredients:

For the Cake:

- 3 eggs
- 200g (1 cup) sugar
- 1 cup plain yogurt
- 1 cup fine semolina
- 1 cup all-purpose flour
- 1 tsp baking powder
- 1 tsp vanilla extract
- Zest of ½ lemon or orange
- 100ml sunflower oil (or neutral oil)
- For the Syrup:
- 1 cup sugar
- 1 cup water
- Juice of ½ lemon

Instructions:

1. Make the Syrup:

   - In a small saucepan, combine sugar and water.
   - Heat over medium heat until the sugar dissolves.
   - Add the lemon juice and bring to a boil.
   - Reduce the heat and simmer for 5–7 minutes.
   - Remove from heat and let it cool to room temperature.

2. Make the Cake Batter:

   - In a mixing bowl, beat the eggs and sugar until light and fluffy.
   - Add yoghurt, oil, vanilla, and lemon/orange zest. Mix well.
   - In another bowl, combine semolina, flour, and baking powder.
   - Gradually mix the dry ingredients into the wet until smooth and thick.

3. Bake the Cake:

   - Preheat oven to 180°C (350°F).
   - Grease a rectangular baking dish (approx. 9×13 in or 20×30 cm).
   - Pour the batter into the dish and smooth the top.
   - Bake for 35–45 minutes, or until golden and a toothpick comes out clean.

4. Soak with Syrup:

- Let the cake cool for 10 minutes.
- While the cake is still warm, slowly pour the cooled syrup evenly over the entire surface.
- Let it rest for at least 2 hours so the syrup absorbs fully.

Serving Suggestions:

- Cut into squares or diamond shapes.

Optional toppings: crushed walnuts, shredded coconut, or a dusting of powdered sugar.

Milk Banitsa

Ingredients:

- 1 pack (400g / ~14 oz) phyllo pastry sheets
- 4 eggs
- 1 litre (4 cups) whole milk
- 200g (1 cup) sugar
- 100g (7 tbsp) unsalted butter (melted)
- 1 tsp vanilla extract or 1 packet vanillin sugar
- Optional: Zest of 1 lemon or orange

Instructions:

1. Preheat the Oven

    - Heat oven to 180°C (350°F).
    - Prepare the Custard
    - In a large bowl, whisk together: Eggs, Sugar, Milk, Vanilla, (Optional) Lemon or orange zest
    - Set aside.

2. Assemble the Banitsa

    - Grease a large baking dish (approx. 9x13 in / 23x33 cm).
    - Roughly cut with hands the phyllo pastry and bake it in the oven for 10-15 minutes until slightly golden.
    - Carefully pour the milk mixture over the whole thing.

Tip: Let it sit for a few minutes so the custard begins to absorb.

3. Bake

    - Bake at 180°C (350°F) for 40–45 minutes, or until golden on top and the custard is set (a knife inserted should come out mostly clean).

4. Cool and serve.

    - Let it cool for at least 15–20 minutes before cutting it.
    - It can be served warm, room temperature, or even chilled.

Baked Apples

Ingredients:

- 4 large apples (firm types like Golden Delicious or Granny Smith)
- 4–6 tbsp granulated sugar (or brown sugar for a deeper flavour)
- 1–2 tsp ground cinnamon
- 2 tbsp chopped walnuts (optional)
- 2 tbsp raisins (optional)
- 1 tbsp butter, cut into small pieces
- ½ cup water (or apple juice for extra flavour)

Instructions:

1. Preheat the oven

    - Set your oven to 180°C (350°F).

2. Prepare the apples

- Wash and core the apples using an apple corer or a knife.
- Don't cut all the way through — leave the bottom intact to hold the filling.
- Place the apples in a small baking dish.

3. Make the filling

In a bowl, mix:

- Sugar, Cinnamon, (Optional) Walnuts and Raisins
- Spoon the filling into the hollow centres of the apples

4. Top with butter

- Place a small piece of butter on top of each filled apple.

5. Bake

- Pour water into the bottom of the baking dish.
- Bake uncovered for 30–40 minutes, or until the apples are soft and caramelised, but not falling apart.

Serving Suggestions:

- Let cool slightly.
- Serve warm, optionally topped with: a dollop of whipped cream, a scoop of vanilla ice cream.
- A drizzle of honey or caramel sauce.

Unique Pastries Cooked In The Whole Area

Buhti

Ingredients:

- 400g all-purpose flour (approximately 3 cups)
- 1 egg
- 250ml Bulgarian yoghurt (about 1 cup)
- 1 tsp baking soda
- 1 tbsp sugar
- 1 pinch of salt
- Sunflower or vegetable oil for frying
- Honey for drizzling (about 100ml)

Instructions:

1. Prepare the Dough:

- In a large mixing bowl, combine the yoghurt and baking soda.
- Stir well and let the mixture sit for a minute to activate the baking soda. It will start to foam.
- Add the egg, sugar, and a pinch of salt to the yoghurt mixture.

- Mix until well combined.
- Gradually add the flour to the mixture, stirring with a wooden spoon or your hands to form a soft dough.
- The dough should be slightly sticky but firm enough to handle.

2. Shape the Buhti:

- Lightly flour your hands and pinch off small portions of dough, rolling them into round or oval shapes about the size of a walnut.
- Alternatively, you can roll the dough on a lightly floured surface and cut it into squares or circles.

3. Heat the Oil:

- Heat about 1–2 cm of sunflower oil in a deep frying pan over medium heat.
- The oil should be hot enough for frying but not smoking.

4. Fry the Buhti:

- Carefully place the shaped dough pieces into the hot oil, frying them in batches.
- Fry each side for 2–3 minutes until golden brown and puffed up.
- Remove the buhti with a slotted spoon and place them on a paper towel-lined plate to drain excess oil.

5. Serve:

- Once all the buhti are fried, transfer them to a serving plate and drizzle generously with honey.
- Serve them warm for the best texture and flavour.

Serving Suggestions:

- Serve Buhti warm, drizzled with honey.

Optional toppings include powdered sugar, jam, or a dollop of yoghurt.

Mekitci

Ingredients:

- 500g (4 cups) all-purpose flour
- 1 packet (7g) dry yeast or 25g fresh yeast
- 250ml (1 cup) lukewarm milk (or water)
- 1 egg
- 1 tbsp of yoghurt
- 1 tsp sugar
- 1 tsp salt
- 2 tbsp oil (plus more for hands and frying)
- Oil for deep frying

Instructions:

1. Activate the Yeast

- Mix the yeast, sugar, and a few tablespoons of lukewarm milk in a small bowl. Let it sit for 5–10 minutes until foamy.

2. Prepare the Dough

In a large bowl, mix:

- Flour, Salt, Activated yeast, Egg, Yoghurt, Remaining lukewarm milk, Oil Knead until you get a soft, elastic dough. It should be slightly sticky but manageable.
- Cover the bowl with a towel and let rise in a warm place for about 1 hour, or until doubled in size.

3. Shape the Mekitsi

- Oil your hands lightly (this prevents sticking).
- Take small pieces of dough (golf-ball size) and stretch them into flat circles about 10–12 cm wide.
- Don't roll — just pull them gently by hand.
- Fry Heat oil (2–3 cm deep) in a wide pan over medium heat.
- Once hot (test with a small piece of dough — it should sizzle), gently place mekitsi into the oil.
- Fry until golden brown on both sides, about 2–3 minutes per side.
- Drain on paper towels.

Serving Suggestions:

- Sprinkle with powdered sugar
- Drizzle with honey
- Serve with fruit jam, Nutella, or white feta cheese and yoghurt

Most Famous Banitsa

Ingredients:

- 1 pack phyllo dough (400–500g / 14–17 oz)
- 300g feta cheese crumbled
- 4 eggs
- 1 cup plain yoghurt
- ½ tsp baking soda (mixed into yoghurt)
- ⅓ cup sunflower oil (or melted butter)
- Optional: 1 egg yolk for brushing the top

Instructions:

1. Preheat the Oven

- Heat oven to 180°C (350°F).

2. Make the Filling

- In a bowl, whisk the eggs.
- Add yoghurt (with baking soda already stirred in).
- Mix in the crumbled cheese and half of the oil.
- Stir everything until well combined.

3. Assemble the Banitsa

- Grease a baking tray (round or rectangular).
- Lay out 2 phyllo sheets at a time, brushing lightly with oil between them.
- Spoon a few tablespoons of the filling on each set of sheets.
- Roll each set loosely or fold accordion-style and place in the tray.
- Repeat until filling and sheets are used up.
- Traditional banitsa is often arranged in a spiral shape (especially in a round pan), but layering or a cylinder shape is also common.

4. Top & Bake

Optional: Brush the top with egg yolk or more oil for a shiny finish.

- A very traditional option is to mix 500ml of sparking water with 2 whole eggs and pour it over the bready layers, and then bake it. It is softer and more moist.
- Bake at 180°C (350°F) for about 40–45 minutes, until golden and crispy.

5. Cool & Serve

- Let it rest for 10–15 minutes before slicing.
- Serve warm, room temperature, or cold.